Behind *the* Scenes
OF *Breast Cancer*

Also by Brenda Ladun

Getting Better, Not Bitter
A Spiritual Prescription for Breast Cancer

Behind the Scenes
OF *Breast Cancer*

A **News Anchor**
Tells **Her Story**
of **Body** and **Soul Recovery**

Brenda Ladun

NEW
HOPE
PUBLISHERS
Birmingham, Alabama

New Hope® Publishers
P. O. Box 12065
Birmingham, AL 35202-2065
www.newhopepublishers.com

New Hope Publishers is a division of WMU®.

Library of Congress Cataloging-in-Publication Data
Ladun, Brenda, 1962-
  Behind the scenes of breast cancer : a news anchor tells her story of
body and soul recovery / Brenda Ladun.
  p. cm.
  ISBN 978-1-59669-091-2 (sc)
  1. Breast—Cancer—Patients—Religious life. 2. Ladun, Brenda, 1962-
3. Breast—Cancer—Religious aspects—Christianity. I. Title.
BV4910.33.L325 2007
248.8'619699449—dc22
    2007014633

ISBN-10: 1-59669-091-7
ISBN-13: 978-1-59669-091-2
N074140 • 0907 • 8M1

Dedication

to my husband, Doug,
and boys,
who are my inspiration!

Table OF Contents

Acknowledgments

RECENTLY MY SISTER LINDA sent me an email that had an inspirational story about geese. The author is unknown, but I know this message came straight from the Lord.

This computer message showed a flock of geese. The message described how their V-formation is no accident. One goose leads and the formation helps to cut the wind resistance so the entire flock moves forward faster. They help each other; when one leader gets tired and falls back, another goose takes the lead and helps the flock move toward its goal. When one goose gets sick and can't go on, two geese stay behind with that one until it revives or dies. Then the two that fell behind join a new flock passing by or try to catch up with the original flock.

These geese cross thousands of miles in all sorts of conditions. Alone they probably wouldn't make it, but together they declare God's awesome glory. How much greater are God's plans for us? We'll never know unless we explore. God teaches us that we can experience amazing accomplishments together, working as a team.

I have to say thanks to my family and friends who, like the geese, helped make this project possible. My husband, Doug Bell, and three wonderful boys, Brooks, Gabby, and Garrett, put up with my writing for many hours and the countless times I said, "I have to write my book!" Thanks for your encouragement, understanding, and patience.

Thanks to my dear friends, sisters, and mother for listening to all the stories and for encouraging me to write them down to share with others.

I'm grateful to my father for showing me there is life beyond this earth.

I thank the Lord Jesus Christ for showing me what love is, and for giving me the desire to pass His love on to heal others.

====

Introduction

YOU MAY WONDER, *How can life go on for a cancer survivor after the ravages of surgery and chemotherapy?* The answer is: hope. That's why I've written this book: to share with you the hope that I found at the beginning of my cancer story, a hope that has continued to blossom even through some of the toughest times of my life. In the five years since I was first diagnosed, I've had an amazing journey of growing in faith. I want to take you behind the scenes, if you will, to share the miracles I've experienced through my life's storms as well as my encounters with others' stories of hope. And I want to share the practical, spiritual lessons I have learned as I have been in recovery—physically and spiritually.

Being a TV news anchor may appear to be a charmed life. But behind the scenes, as everyone learns, there are ups and downs, deaths, sicknesses, and other struggles in this life. I've learned over the past five years that the important thing in life is not necessarily the problem, but how I react to the problem. Do I *trust* God? Or do I get mad at Him and reject His love? Or do I submit to His will, pray, pray some more, trust Him more, give Him honor and glory, and hold on to my joy in Him?

Sure, life is full of potholes, but I'm convinced we've been put here to learn and grow and glorify God through our actions. You may wonder how I'm certain this life has something to do with growing in faith and grace. I have battled cancer with Him and I have survived. I'm a living, breathing testimony that it's not only possible, but also fruitful to have a personal relationship with the Lord Jesus Christ and to be an overcomer through God.

Do miracles happen today? As a journalist, allow me to present you with the facts and let you decide. Does God answer prayer? I only know that when I pray sincere, specific prayers, He answers them specifically, and He makes the supernatural and wonderful happen. I trust Him. I stand in awe of God and His wonders. He speaks to me and fills me with joy, and He will speak to each one of us if we let Him. God loves us so much. He put us here for a purpose.

By sharing my life with you, I hope to share how I became more open to God's love. He wants to have a real relationship with each one of us. But watch out if you believe; be ready for the ride of your life. Come along and join me in the amazement I feel about how God works.

=======================

Thank You, Lord, for allowing me more precious time, surviving these years. Thank You for the assurance of knowing that when we leave here, You'll carry us home to heaven. Thank You for that assurance that the ones we love who have passed on can live forever with You!

Chapter One

Good News: God Is in Control

He lifted me out of the pit of despair, out of the mud and the mire. He set my feet on solid ground and steadied me as I walked along. He has given me a new song to sing, a hymn of praise to our God. Many will see what he has done and be amazed. They will put their trust in the Lord.

—Psalm 40:2–3

How do I *know* God is in control? I'm a living witness to His power over breast cancer and every other issue in my life. As if this were not enough, God has inundated me with amazing stories of His control in others' lives; this huge wave of healing encouragement has swept me closer to Him. These testimonies about what God is doing—how He is moving in our midst—are a significant part of my healing. Through these testimonies, I have become vividly aware of God's comfort and one of its purposes: "He comforts us in all our troubles so that we can comfort others. When they are troubled, we will be able to give them the same comfort God has given us" (2 Corinthians 1:4). My prayer is that you, too, will be blessed with His awesome comfort as you go behind the scenes with me to see His hand at work.

Yes, I've got "a new song in my mouth": I have overcome the devastation of breast cancer for more than five years now, and I add my voice to the chorus of those who praise God for His help and goodness! This has been a challenging season in my life, my family's lives, and for many with whom I have interacted, whose stories I share here. But this really is God's story. When I thought I was finished writing, He was not done with it.

As with my first book *Getting Better, Not Bitter* (2002), which is about coping with the initial breast cancer diagnosis and surgery, I expected the editor to this new manuscript to tell me to make finishing touches, and that would be it. I breathed a sigh of relief when I turned in my story about all of the new experiences I've encountered as a five-year cancer survivor. But something very unusual began to unfold on the Friday morning after I thought I had finished writing, and it has astounded me.

The phone rang. It was Vickie Imbusch, asking if my middle son could spend the night with her son.

"Vickie, I know he is planning to run in my Conquer Cancer run tomorrow. Can we do it another week?"

"Sure!" She completely understood. "But Brenda, I

still want to go to coffee. I have so much to tell you."

"Tell me a little now if you have time?" I asked.

She went on to share a vision she had had of Jesus. The Lord led her to tell me that particular morning about this vision that would help lead her through a faith walk during a battle with cancer.

I told Vickie I wanted to include her story in my book and would pray that the publisher would allow it. Here's the kicker: The same morning, the editor was in a meeting with a group that wanted more content. So when the editor got my email asking if I could add more pages, she jumped for joy. It would not be the last time that God would encourage and comfort me with the testimonies of others.

Walking into work at my news job at ABC 33/40, Birmingham, Alabama, I heard a story that made everyone say, "Wow!". In short, Libby Ashley thought she was having a breast cancer recurrence. She prayed for Jesus to keep His hand on her until she was sure she was healed. Then an x-ray she had came back with a mystery hand on it—no bones appeared—but the x-ray showed markings on the hand and wrist that Libby believes are nail holes.

There's more. I had a conversation with a TV producer that led to the story of her sister's miraculous healing from a breast cancer recurrence—which had metastasized to her brain, bones, optic nerve, and liver. That story connected me to the sister's prayer group where I learned about a miracle of a child healed from a brain tumor and serious complications. The tumor simply shrank! Her mother, Kim Benos, gives glory to God, saying it's been ten years and her child has no symptoms. A former oncology nurse, Kim says sometimes people are healed with chemo or other treatments and prayer, and other times by the power of prayer.

Not too long after that, on a stormy Valentine's Day, I couldn't go home after the 6:00 P.M. news for dinner with my husband and boys. We anchors were on standby to report storm damage if necessary. Later, I decided I needed to get some Valentine's goodies for the family, so I dashed into a nearby grocery store. I heard someone gasp and I looked up. It was Kim. She said she rarely shopped there. We laughed and exchanged more stories of how God has controlled what happens in our lives.

While looking at the Valentine cards, a man said hello and introduced himself as Joe Rosenthal. He said we had met years ago, but I couldn't remember where. When I headed to check out, there Joe was again. He chatted and then went on to talk spontaneously about blessings. "My daughter has been healed of seizures. She's been seizure-free for three years. We know it's a miracle." That big wave swept me up again. It can only be explained as God's control, and what an encouragement it is to my soul.

Then there was that Sunday morning when I felt led to go down to the front of the church and talk with our pastor, Buddy Gray, after service, to tell him, "I know you have a heavy load and I am praying for you."

He thanked me and said, "A woman is planning to start a breast-cancer survivor ministry here at Hunter Street. I will get you in touch with her."

A voice from his right said, "I'm right here!" The woman the pastor was talking about had also felt led to come down front that Sunday. When I talked with this lovely, young, breast cancer survivor standing next to Buddy, she said to me, "Perhaps you would want to lead this ministry?" I felt strongly this was her calling, told her so, and saw the confirmation in her eyes. This meeting had been orchestrated by God's Holy Spirit.

I felt led to a certain restaurant after church that we hadn't been to in years. There, I met an old friend and nurse who happened to have the right connections for someone I was praying for to get the job he desperately needed. Both of us agreed it was God who had arranged this odd meeting; He led us to the restaurant at the same moment. It was no coincidence that Pastor Gray's sermon earlier that day had been about loving our neighbor as ourselves. This meeting helped to answer my prayer.

Why Worry?

If you look, you may not be able to understand it, but you can recognize God's tapestry in how He has ordered our lives and orchestrated our circumstances to help one another, no matter what difficulties we face and endure.

I find the more I reach out to help others, the more I'm blessed in return. Although that's not the reason for reaching out, it's a side effect, and a good one. And I'm thankful for those who have reached out to comfort me.

If God clearly is in control of my life, what do I have to worry about anyway? Nothing! He'll handle it all. As a Christian, there is nothing to fear. Not even death! I've let go of fear, anxiety, and depression. Why not celebrate life and find the joy in trusting in His sovereignty, no matter the outcome? Well, there is the issue of our *need* for control.

I don't know about you, but I have been a control freak! I still have this deep-seated need to fix everything for everyone. When I'm in a shopping mall and someone I don't know drops something 20 yards down the mall, I want to rush and help that person pick it up. I struggle not to do everything for everyone. I was recently at a restaurant where the waitress looked tired and not very excited to be there. I asked her how she was doing. She said it had been a long week!

"I'm so tired and I'm supposed to do a double shift."

I wanted to jump up and help her clear her table. I thought to myself, *I'll be your celebrity waiter and give you the rest of the day off.* But then I looked at my children sitting at the table with our friends, and I knew it was a little silly. Is it a control thing? I think so. I have a need to fix it all. But guess what? God keeps reminding me that He's the greatest fixer of them all. Not me. I have to let Him lead.

Speaking of trying not to lead, this reminds me of the time I agreed to be a celebrity dancer for an exhibition and fund-raiser for senior citizens. It was a local version of *Dancing with the Stars*. I had to take some dance lessons and realized how bad this whole control thing is. I simply had trouble letting the dance instructor lead! What a pain I must have been. When I finally realized that I would just mess up the dance and the whole thing that was designed for seniors, I gave up control. It was one of the most fun experiences I've had! I later learned that my instructor was Fabian Sanchez, the US Mambo Champion. I'm glad I let him lead!

What if we all let God lead like we are in a beautiful dance with Him? Wouldn't that be the most secure, relaxing, and beautiful experience? What a great way to go through life. Who can you trust more not to drop you? God! He literally and figuratively won't let you down. And even though there are painful experiences we'll face in this life, He loves us and intends them for good.

But being a mother of three boys, it's hard to let go sometimes. I feel as if it's all up to me to get things done, make sure the boys are accomplished at school, and so on. But God has spoken to me about this, letting me know that I have a form of pride. "'God opposes the proud but favors the humble.' So humble yourselves before God. Resist the devil, and he will flee from you" (James 4:6–7). Is that what I'd been doing most of my life? Being proud that I could handle everything on my own? I think so! God continues to open my eyes. Thank You, Lord. Trying to be the perfect wife, mom, daughter, TV news anchor, and all-around person . . . was I submitting to the Lord's control? Not enough, that's for sure. Every day, being a recovering type-A personality, I try to turn it all over to God. I must admit, though, some days I'm more successful than others.

One of the good things about cancer is that it gave me a chance to regroup, look at my life, and make changes I need to make because of the lessons I have learned. I'm sad for people who die suddenly and don't get the chance to do so, or to say goodbye. Over the years, there were times I thought a recurrence might be happening. That's when I'd stop in my tracks and say, thinking to myself, *Oh, Lord, am I really living the way I promised you I'd live? Am I finding your joy in each day?*

Turning It Over to God

Since my breast cancer diagnosis, undergoing a double mastectomy, reconstruction, and chemotherapy, I vowed to take time to do the little important activities with my kids, like taking a bike ride when there were still dishes in the sink. I'd work on doing more fun trips, and not worry so much about a rip in the sofa.

I realized how wonderful it is that I survived long

enough to see my youngest son learn to ride a bike without training wheels. Moments like this are a little piece of heaven for me. In fact, every Mother's Day, I bawl like a baby because I've lived to see one more.

On one particularly lovely spring day, I decided to leave my house in the dust—literally—to let go, and ride a bike with my youngest son. He was six years old at the time.

Being the youngest of three boys, it's amazing how Garrett picks up how to do something more easily because he's been observing his older brothers. One day, he decided he was done with the training wheels on his little bike, and wanted to try his brother's big bike. He hopped on, and to the family's amazement, it only took one push and he was off—very little, if any, wobbling occurred. But he could only go one speed—fast—in order to control his wobbles.

"Hey, Garrett, wait for me!" I shouted.

But there was no slowing him down. I guess he figured if he did slow down, he'd fall over. So it was off to the races with Garrett. I was so proud of him. No falling, pure speed. As I looked at him go, I remembered a story my mother told me about myself as a baby. She said, "You just took off running! You never walked."

Like Garrett, I was the youngest. I watched my two older sisters closely and then, bang!, took off. I've been like that ever since, just a-runnin'! Yes, Garrett is a lot like I used to be, anxious to show the world he is able to control things himself! But that day, after a little while, I told Garrett to slow down! "OK, it's time to turn around!"

He did, and raced back toward the house to our backyard separated by a creek and a rickety bridge. It's been weathered in many wicked Alabama storms. One part of the railing is gone because a fallen tree once crashed into it. I watched my little son with pride and said to myself, *He's amazing. He just started riding.* I saw him heading to the damaged bridge, peddling at a good rate of speed. It was then that I started to yell, "Garrett! Stop there!"

Whew, just about that time, he rolled to a stop on the bridge, short of falling into the creek. But then he took both feet off the ground and, you guessed it, the bike rolled 12 more inches, far enough for the wheel to catch the edge of the wood, causing the bike—and Garrett with it—to tumble into the rocky creek below. I gasped. "Garrett, are you OK?" I yelled. No answer, only silence. I knew that since it hadn't rained in quite a while, he and his bike only had a rocky landing meeting them at the bottom of the dry waterway.

"Garrett!" I screamed, threw my bike down, and ran to the creek. There he was shuffling to get up, one shoe on, one shoe off, and his helmet cockeyed. He had the look of surprise and shock, while still trying to be cool.

"I'm good," he said as he reached for my hand to help pull him out. He had a nasty brush-burn on his leg. I could only deduce that was where his leg brushed against the wooden plank of the bridge floor, as he plunged to the rocks below.

"Garrett . . . I was so scared . . . and you didn't answer me." I said.

"Well," Garrett said with the attitude of a 50-year-old man, "I thought I was looking at a snake next to my eye and I wanted to be very quiet so he wouldn't bite me. But it wasn't a snake at all," he said matter-of-factly. "It was a fish about this long." His forefinger and thumb made the distance of about three inches.

I wrapped my arms around him and said, "Honey, I'm so sorry. Are you all right?" At that point I was ready for the tears and the screams of horror for what he'd been through. After our embrace, I pulled back and to my surprise, he was giggling.

I said. "You really are a tough guy!"

God Holds Us in His Hands

"God is our refuge and strength, always ready to help in times of trouble. So we will not fear when earthquakes come and the mountains crumble into the sea" (Psalm 46:1–2). This brush with disaster was another reminder I am not in control. That fall could have gone either way that day; he could have suffered a serious head injury, or back injury. It was by the grace of God that Garrett had only a few scratches. God again showed me that He had Garrett *and* me in the palm of His hands on this day, and certainly every day!

Recently, I felt like God grabbed me again by the shoulders to remind me that life is a good gift from Him. New tests had been developed in the five years since my tumor was removed. I'd been waiting a month for the results of what was supposed to be a two-week test. During my five-year checkup (that I'd planned would be nothing but a celebration), my oncologist Dr. Cantrell reviewed the facts of my case. I had been stage two, which means the cancer had started invading the rest of my body. I had an aggressive tumor, and I was hormone-receptor positive; all reasons according to Doc that I should probably have an *oophorectomy* (ovaries removed) and take more medicine to suppress any tiny cancer cells.

But at the age of 44, this would not be easy. I wouldn't be able to take hormones. After all, they were trying to reduce hormones in my body. So I'd be off hormones cold turkey—which also would mean instant menopause. Some women indicated to me that the outcome wouldn't be pretty. So I consulted with my gynecologist, Dr. Elizabeth Snowden, who recommended holding off or avoiding the surgery, if possible. There it was, cancer, slapping me in the face again, even though my blood was clean. I felt my heart rate quicken. Fear and anxiety were back.

But Dr. Cantrell offered yet another option— another test that could tell us if I was at high risk or low risk for recurrence. The test would analyze my tumor, which had been kept in a lab. A certain chemical makeup would tell us how likely it was for the cancer to return.

I'd been healed by the Lord; I almost felt as though agreeing to the test meant I was being unfaithful. However, a low risk would get old Doc off my back about having more surgery and I was all for that. Also, being a mother of three, I felt I needed to do everything I could to stay healthy.

So without having to roll up a sleeve, the old tumor—which had been kept in the lab for ten years—was poked and prodded. I had a great mental image of beating it up. *Take that, you old cancer.* Not that this would do any good. I'd already defeated the tumor with the Lord's help.

This would be an expensive test. It cost a couple thousand dollars and we'd have to grapple with the insurance probably. Though Dr. Cantrell said insurance should cover it in the end. But the idea of the test brought back butterflies in my stomach. What would it reveal? I prayed that the Lord again would handle this as He had all the other parts of the cancer struggle. It's just that it seemed to dredge up some of the feelings and "What if?" questions all over again. I had wanted to put all that behind me. But there I was, facing the reality of fighting cancer.

The test results were supposed to be in within a couple of days. Then that turned into weeks. It was a hang-up with the insurance. Assurances from Dr.

Cantrell seemed to work. The test was finally in. I'd hoped to get a quick review over the phone. I'd hoped to hear, "Little or no chance of recurrence, it's over; you're done." But I didn't hear that on the phone from the nurse. She said, "Dr. Cantrell wants to see you to go over the results of the test." In recent history, phone calls like that were never good.

So my knight in shining armor went along with me that day to help slay the dragons; Doug, my sweet husband, marched into the office. Neither of us knew what we'd hear. We hoped and prayed for some good news.

Dr. Cantrell came in smiling. He was a hero in the war on cancer; he'd beaten back many a cancer cell in his time. I imagined his victories and defeats along the way.

"Well, the test shows you are in a gray area," he announced.

"What does that mean?" I asked.

"It means, you're not in a high risk for recurrence . . . but you're not in a low risk either." He said. "It means we'll hold off on surgery."

No surgery. That was good news, but I felt like this expensive test still left me hanging. That meant I was in a nebulous gray area and they didn't really know if I'd have a recurrence or not. *Thank you, modern science!* But then I realized I had been putting my hope in a science test that hadn't been on the market very long, instead of putting my hope and trust in my sovereign God. I almost burst out into laughter. It's what I'd thought all along: *I should trust the Lord.* The Lord sure seems to have a sense of humor. All that worry and wondering and there I was back where I had started, trusting in God's power over my health. Yes, the Lord really is in control. My future is in His hands. I'll admit it, though—I have been a slow learner.

Worship Study Questions

•What is it in my life that I need to surrender to God's control?

_____

_____

_____

_____

•How will I change my life to really surrender to Him?

_____

_____

_____

_____

_____

•How could my life change if I let Him lead me?

_____

_____

_____

_____

Chapter Two

Prayer Power Tools

Are any of you suffering hardships? You should pray. Are any of you happy? You should sing praises. Are any of you sick? You should call for the elders of the church to come and pray over you, anointing you with oil in the name of the Lord. Such a prayer offered in faith will heal the sick, and the Lord will make you well. And if you have committed any sins, you will be forgiven. Confess your sins to each other and pray for each other so that you may be healed. The earnest prayer of a righteous person has great power and produces wonderful results.

—James 5:13–16

WHY AM I SURPRISED when God answers prayers? Why don't I pray constantly? Why do I pray more intensely during a crisis? Wouldn't life be better if

I prayed sincerely about all things? Doesn't it say in the Word to pray without ceasing?

God promises in His Word that He will answer our prayers. I will admit, the answers aren't always exactly what I want. But as I look back on my life and dealing with cancer and other struggles, the Lord has answered me in many ways. He's also revealed how he has answered the prayers of others. By combining my testimony with the testimony of others, I can see a small portion of how grand and wonderful God is. Prayer is worshipping, talking, and having a relationship with our Lord, a relationship for which I am grateful

There I was, in my bathroom getting ready for that six-month checkup to find out if the cancer had stayed away. Even a year out, these checkups were nerve-racking. I remember trying to stay upbeat. But sometimes I'd feel a little irritable. *Why did I have to do this?* Part of me wanted to rush in and throw my arm out and say, "OK, tell me everything is alright and that I'll never have to worry again." Of course that is ridiculous, because doctors don't know. That's the reason for the checkups. The other part of me wanted to run far away from another test. I was praying for the Lord to take the worry about a possible recurrence away from me.

Lord you've carried me this far; get me through the test. Also allow the blood to flow so that I'll only be poked once, not five times. The chemo had damaged my veins on my left arm, and my right arm had lymph nodes out to search for the spread of cancer, so in order to prevent the arm from swelling, I wasn't supposed to get poked or have blood pressure checks on that arm again. My lymphatic system was also weak because I had 16 lymph nodes removed so that surgeons could test for signs of cancer.

Lymph nodes are tiny little sacks all over our bodies that help catch disease, fight it, and clean our skin of impurities. God is amazing how He's provided so much in our bodies to care for us. Before cancer, I never even knew anything about a lymph node.

By the grace of God, I was feeling calm and confident after that prayer. I was OK! I would be able to walk into the oncologist's office without feeling like making a run for the border. Then suddenly I heard a frantic knock at the bathroom door.

"Mommy! Daddy mad!"

"What is it, Garrett? I asked my youngest. He was three years old at the time.

"Daddy mad!"

"Why dear?"

"Whaa'," was the only answer I got. So I went to investigate myself.

I found my husband flapping his arms and saying, "I'm going to tell my mother on you!" He referred to the kids. That's right; a grown man was threatening to call Grandma to tattle on his own offspring!

I said, "What's going on here?!"

Brooks, my nine-year-old, said, "Mom, Garrett threw the Spider-Man watch in the hole!"

I said, "The hole. What hole?!"

"The hole in the wall."

"The hole in the wall? What hole in the wall?!" My voice was getting louder.

Garrett, like many other children at that age, became fascinated with opening and closing the back door. He had discovered the doorstop and didn't see that it had much use. So he politely unscrewed it from the wall and tossed it aside. Then the game of swinging the door open and closed was more fun. He literally got a real bang out of it, especially when the door knob hit the drywall. *Boom*: what a great, powerful sound for a child. But the result was the door handle crashing through the wall leaving a clean hole the size of a large plum near my back door.

Now, let me explain the significance of the watch. Grandma Bell, my husband's mother, had saved little coupons from the corners of cracker boxes for months. She was so proud she had finally saved up enough for the boys' Spider-Man watches. Then we waited for them to arrive. Finally, they did arrive—all two of them. We have three boys! We all figured Garrett couldn't tell time and was so young he wouldn't really care about the Spiderman watch, right? Wrong! So you see, Garrett politely deposited the Spiderman watch he didn't get into his hole in the wall. I wonder if, in his little three-year-old brain, he'd figured he really got one over on us!

About that time, I realized I had to leave for my doctor's appointment. I was actually looking forward to going to the doctor at this point! "Gee guys, I'm so sorry I have to leave to go to see Dr. Cantrell. But how about if you straighten out a hanger and put some chewed chewing gum on the end of it and fish it out? Sorry, gotta go!" I said almost gleefully, knowing I had an escape hatch out of the house of chaos on this day at least. So I hopped in the car feeling relieved to be out of there.

But when I stopped at a red light and glanced over at the seat where I usually put my purse, I was aghast. It wasn't there! Was I driving without a license? I looked all around the car. No purse. Uh oh! You know what happens on the day you don't have your driver's license, don't you? You get stopped by a police officer or you get into a fender bender. Then you're in bigger trouble! I had to go back into the house of chaos. I thought, *maybe I can just sneak in and grab the purse and go.* No. I walked in and they were all lined up by the front door. Each one had a huge Cheshire cat grin.

"So," I said, "did the chewing gum and hanger work?"

"No," my husband replied, still showing his pearly whites.

Brooks, my nine-year-old at the time, pointed to his father. Doug had a hammer in one hand and a butter knife in the other. You guessed it. We then had two holes in the wall!

Prayer, Scripture, and Surrender

That story reminds me how God gives us all we need to get through every situation in life, if we only choose to access His power. The Lord Jesus Christ helped me through cancer, deaths in the family, jobs struggles, and more. The first key is to let God lead. It can't be the other way around. Each day I learn that, with God's help, nothing is impossible.

Next, God leads the way and provides His tools, such as digging into Scripture and praying, to yield a richer, more meaningful, and more content life. And the good Lord continues to remind me I need to surrender to Him on a daily basis. Oh sure, going through cancer, I surrendered. I had to do so. I couldn't handle it on my own. But as I grew stronger and more self-sufficient, I didn't want to lose the sweet lessons the Lord taught me through the cancer experience: "Be still, and know that I am God!" (Psalm 46:10).

Many people assume that once you are past the cancer, life is a breeze. For me, nothing compared to the feelings of going through the fight for life. But after the battle with cancer, a job loss, the death of my father, and the death of fellow friends with cancer were some of my uphill battles. But behind the scenes of each struggle, the Lord held us, molded us, encouraged us, and led us to new spiritual heights. I can see how He used the cancer experience to help me get through future crisis situations.

As running or walking up a hill makes you stronger physically, God strengthened me through hard times. Many cancer survivors I've talked to agree: The skies are a little bluer, sunsets are more beautiful, and life is sweeter when we allow God to reveal our blessings to us through our difficulties. It's when you are about to lose something that everything seems more precious. Facing the loss of life makes every breath and every moment with loved ones incredibly special and sweet because we have been faced with death.

It reminds me of the story of the quarrelsome old couple. He had had a heart attack. She didn't know if he would live through the night. They had for years sniped at each other. But on this night . . . their love for each other had been revived and renewed . . . because each of them thought it was over. You could hear, "Honey," this and "Sweetie, you're so wonderful!" that. Mushy, lovey-dovey stuff. But the minute the doctor told them he would be OK . . . they returned to their game of sniping at each other.

That's what I hope doesn't happen to me. I pray I will remember the lesson God taught me through cancer and I won't go back to the old way of not appreciating life. But in five years, with three kids and heavy sports schedules, homework, a traveling husband and a career... I'm often faced with God's mirror. I have to be honest. I don't always react the way I wish I would. But time and time again, there's the Lord, the great

Shepherd . . . herding me back to His way.

The five-years-past-cancer challenge is to hold on to the lessons the Lord has taught. Life has a way of getting busy again. It has a way of rolling along. And it also has many of the same potholes that I fell in before. Let's face it; life is not perfect. But learning to lean more and more on the Lord Jesus Christ has constantly reassured me. He's always there when I'm ready to fall, fear, or give up. He continually renews my strength and even in the hardest times, the Lord has delivered joy and blessings as I pray, turn to His Word, and surrender to Him. "But those who trust in the LORD will find new strength. They will soar high on wings like eagles. They will run and not grow weary. They will walk and not faint" (Isaiah 40:31).

God also used cancer to show me that I could slow down and say no—so that I can be still before Him. "But LORD, be merciful to us, for we have waited for you. Be our strong arm each day and our salvation in times of trouble" (Isaiah 33:2). God caused cancer to make me stronger in a lot of ways. For example, I notice many moms are stressed out because all their children are overcommitted. Their lives are faster than high-speed Internet. Part of the charm of years gone by was that people had time to go fishing. Today it's dance lessons, baseball, basketball, football, and more.

This year, for the first year, I decided not to make myself crazy with activity. We didn't participate in Scouts and the boys took off the basketball season for the first time in years. In fact, this is our first break *ever* for a season of sports. Do I regret it? Not at all. We are enjoying Saturday mornings together!

Partners in Prayer

Even though I'm familiar with the power of God, each time He makes His presence known, I stand in awe. I was heading to another six-month checkup. The nurse would extract the blood and send it off to a lab to determine if that nasty little cancer decided to raise its ugly little cell again? OK, time to pray. *Lord, let it be alright. Let the cancer stay away.* I ran and asked my running buddies to pray (more like sisters in Christ, but also known as the Hoover Gazelles, or the thundering herd). We often pray for one another. In fact, the running group was a result of prayer.

That morning, while jogging before dawn, I let them in on my little secret. I said, "Hey, you guys, you know I prayed for you."

Someone said, "I know, we always pray for each other." They agreed to pray for the test. But that day I didn't ask that the blood flow freely. It's always a challenge. I wonder if I'm more turnip than human since cancer. The chemo-damaged arteries don't want to give up the blood.

I said, "No, I mean I prayed for good, godly women in my life that I could run with and that I could learn from and find Christian encouragement." Without raising an eyebrow, all five of us had shared that each one of us had prayed the same exact prayer! The Lord had, indeed, brought us together. No one could ever convince me that our group was an accident or a coincidence. We have been there through heartaches, deaths, family crises, obstinate children, and even lost dogs. Basically, the running and talking has been an encouragement and we remind each other that the Lord will guide us. On this morning, I asked for a good result on my test and ignored the blood-flow issue.

I came back home from my run, showered, and got ready for the doctor's appointment. It was summer so there was no school to worry about. The kids were plunked in front of the television watching their favorite cartoon.

I drank lots of water and juice, trying to plump up those veins so the blood would make its much anticipated appearance. I've been accused by my family that I am not human, because I stay up late, get up early and run, and go, go, go all day. When people ask me how I do it, I tell them it's the Lord. There is no other explanation. Sometimes when the blood was being elusive, I'd wonder, am I human? But we all know better. The blood is there!

I called my mother on the way, to ask for prayer about the test, as I always had. She is a powerful prayer partner. I always say she has a "direct line" to our Lord. She assured me she would be in prayer that morning. So I walked in with confidence the Lord would be, indeed, on my side. I sat in the waiting room and looked at all the people from different walks of life. All these people with one of the most important things in common: their health. We all had been touched by cancer.

These were my brothers and sisters in the fight. We all felt the shock, the pangs of fear, and the over-whelming moments. I prayed that they, too, wouldn't feel defeated but instead empowered by the Holy Spirit and molded for good. I've made many friendships in that waiting room. There's something reassuring when I spend time with a fellow cancer survivor. We don't have to put on airs; we know where we are coming from. All the outward appearances—hair, nails, fancy cars, furniture (and so on)—take a backseat to fighting for your life. So many cancer patients I've met have a spiritual depth that is almost indescribable and com-forting to be around.

"Brenda?" The nurse called.

It was my time. I had to weigh in to make sure I hadn't lost or gained too much weight, which could indicate cancer again. I was proud of maintaining my weight because everyone said I'd gain a lot of weight on the drug Tamoxifen, which is supposed to suppress cancer growth. In fact, the chemo and the steroids were supposed to cause weight gain and bloating. But the Lord led me to exercise and drink a lot of water as well as eat right. That all helped carry me through without being defeated by major weight gain.

I worked hard to stay fit and get stronger. I walked, jogged, ran, played tennis, biked, swam, and ate fresh fruit and vegetables. I share my diet and fitness plan in the DVD about getting your life back after breast cancer that accompanies this book. Study after study finds women who exercise after a cancer diagnosis live longer, not to mention they feel better. The scale showed I weighed less than 120 pounds, and that felt good!

"Are you still running?" the friendly nurse asked.

Yes" I replied. "I ran six miles this morning."

"Wow!" She said. "Not bad!"

Then it was time for the extraction of the life-giving blood from my body. The nurses were kind and called for the butterfly needle, one of the smallest, usually used for children. My veins were small to begin with, and the chemo had complicated the matter by burning them. So there we went digging for red gold. Nope, didn't hit it the first time or the second time either. The third, fourth, and fifth times weren't fruitful. The human pincushion was starting to feel faint. I excused myself, went to the bathroom, and splashed cold water on my face. I said a prayer and returned to the recliner. The friendly nurse poked me one more time in a different vein. I imagined she didn't like this process any better than me and I apologized for being a difficult patient. *Ahhh, there, a little came out, not much but a little.*

The kind nurse had mercy on me. She offered, "I'm going to ask the lab to work with this. It's not much but hopefully it will be enough to get what we're looking for."

I sprang from the chair. I met with Dr. James Cantrel, my oncologist and one of my heroes in my cancer battle. The initial tests looked good. The liver function is always something they look at and that was good. But as usual, I was told we'd have to wait a day or so for the cancer check test. And that's always been a challenge. Trying to grocery shop, pack lunches, attend school functions, and work anchoring the news, while in the back of my mind wondering when I'd get my test back and what it would reveal. Although I pray and put it in Gods hands, I do like to hear I'm in the clear!

As I headed home from my appointment, I had that freeing, uplifting feeling. *Well, I did it. I won't have to repeat this for another six months.* I was about to hum on the way up the highway when I got the call.

"Hello, Brenda?" said the sweet nurse on the other end of the line. "I really hate to tell you this . . ."

Oh no, had they gotten bad results so soon?

"We didn't get enough blood for the test. You'll have to come back in. We can do it another day if you like?"

Noooooo! I thought this couldn't be! I was just celebrating my freedom and now I had to go back. *Do it another day? Are you kidding?* I thought. I wanted this behind me so I could move on to the next challenge.

"No, I'll be right back. Thank you." My jaw dropped in disbelief. Next, I did what most children do in a crisis: I called my momma!

"Hey, Mom. I forgot to ask you to pray about something on my test. Please pray that the blood will flow." I prayed with my mother right then and there. You won't believe what happened next!

No Coincidences

While on the highway, after I turned the car around to go back to the oncologist's office, a car seemed to come from out of nowhere and swerved toward me. I veered into a parking lot and avoided what would have been a very bad crash. That car was about to hit right on the driver's side. I said, "Yikes! Mom, I gotta go!"

When my car came to a stop in what was thankfully an empty parking lot, my heart was pounding in my chest—I could hear it in my ears beating. I gasped for breath. Wow, that got the old blood flowing!

I called my mom back to say, "I'm OK, but I almost had a car crash into me. They never saw me and just pushed me to the side of the road." If there had been a telephone pole there instead of a parking lot, I might not be writing this today! Oh, the Lord is good. I hung up with Mom as she was praising Jesus for my safety.

Whew, that was close! I thought. *God really is good!* I realized what a baby I had been. I figured my tense arm while trying to get the blood extracted probably restricted my blood flow. Well it was pumping now! I asked for God to forgive me for not completely trusting Him during my blood test and being filled with fear. I asked Him to allow the blood to flow—not through a car accident, mind you—but through the butterfly needle into the tube for testing.

Like a good soldier, I marched back into my least favorite chair and held out my arm. But this time, the blood spurted into the tube and flowed freely. It was like a geyser I had seen as a child out west. Hallelujah! Praise God! But this is also a reminder that God does answer specific prayer. I also feel He has a sense of humor. That close call in the car got my heart pumping and I guess helped get the blood moving.

I know: "I can do all things through Christ who strengthens me" (Philippians 4:13 NKJV). I have to remember and trust that fact in all stressful situations. Just like the blood test, I need to remember to pray about everything. It seems the Lord continues to mold me and strengthen my faith and teach me daily: "I have refined you, but not as silver is refined. Rather, I have refined you in the furnace of suffering" (Isaiah 48:10).

I pray in the car regularly, because it seems I'm always in the car. And after that close call you can easily understand why I need His angels surrounding my car. I drive a lot; two trips to school to drop off kids five days a week, and extra trips for school activities, football, baseball games, and practices. Then there are the trips to work, home for dinner to spend quality time with the kids and Doug, and then back to work.

So I have a quiet time with God in the car on many days. Of course most of us should pray in the car continuously for protection, wisdom, and a cool head.

Before cancer, I never thought to pray for my own health, but now I do. I always prayed for my kid's health and protection, but not for my own. Now that I realize the power of prayer is so real, I think we should probably get on our knees for most of the day.

One lesson God taught me through cancer I never want to forget. Situations like the bloodless blood test and near-crash remind me that prayer works. Simply taking specific requests to Him in earnest prayer is so important. Once we understand we are able to access such great power, it can blow our minds.

But since I surrendered to God while lying on the bed waiting to go into surgery, I know I'll be going home to heaven when I die because of His grace; it's a win-win situation. Once we understand and fully digest that fact, we can sit back and relax on the beach of life, so to speak. How our perspective changes when we can look at the troubles of this world and fully understand and expect something better when we pass from here! But while we are here, it's easy to be blind to the greatness of God unless we open our hearts up to what His grace means to us every day. One way to access that understanding is to pray.

God wants to hear from us about every aspect of our lives, and we're not bothering Him. He wants to be a part of our day. I've learned through cancer to pray about everything. Do I pray every time I have to make a decision? No, I have to admit I slip. But I can tell there is a difference from when I pray about a decision and when I don't. When I pray about decisions or actions in my life, things work out better. When I return to my type-A days, and try to control everything and fix everything, things don't go well at all. When I think I can do things all on my own, I often feel like I'm trudging up a mountain in a blinding snowstorm against the wind. Even if it's a simple thing that I didn't pray about, it can turn into the most complicated trial I've ever been through.

God answers prayer. Not always the way we conceive He will answer, but He does answer according to His will. Sometimes He heals here on earth and sometimes in heaven. The more I study the reality of heaven, I think the real sorrow is for those of us left here on earth, who continue to face disease, crime, and hardships, while our loved ones in heaven are in a greater and perfect place.

Did I pray for healing during my cancer battle? Yes. I specifically asked Him for healing. I also surrendered my life and everything about it into God's hands and that felt good. Many others were praying for me as well. And it's amazing what God did.

Worship Study Questions

•What is it I need to pray about?

_____

_____

_____

_____

•Do I pray anxious prayers or do I truly believe God will do what He says He will do?

_____

_____

_____

_____

•How will I change my prayer life to draw closer to Him?

_____

_____

_____

_____

Chapter Three

Supernatural Healing

If we are unfaithful, he remains faithful, for he cannot deny who he is.

—2 Timothy 2:13

MY BATTLE WITH BREAST CANCER not only has truly invigorated my prayer life; but also the ordeal has deepened my Bible reading and other spiritual disciplines. It also has opened my mind and heart to understand that God is almighty and operates outside my understanding. He is supernatural; He operates in ways we cannot explain. In this chapter, I will share an unusual example—not for God, but for me—of His supernatural power in my life. I want to do this to glorify God and His power. God has let me know that others have experienced this phenomenon too.

One day after prayer, I was in my bedroom and I felt an electrical surge go through my body. I thought:

What was that!? Was it God's answer to my prayer? Was it a side effect from the chemo? I couldn't get anyone to say that a random surge through the body is related to the chemo. I asked my oncologist about it and my sister, the nurse who had been talking me through the side effects of chemo, but neither one had an answer. I thought perhaps it was the nerve endings healing. But a couple of years after that, I had three other stories from other cancer survivors who'd had a similar experience after intense prayer. They believe that surge was God's supernatural healing. Each one had serious battles and it's nothing less than miraculous that they are alive today.

Pat Lee is a very dear friend. I received a phone call from Pat that let me know she was going to be a very special part of my life. "Brenda, the doctor says I have breast cancer," she said. Those words rang in my ears like a giant gong! *It wasn't true, was it?* Around that time, a number of people were being diagnosed. It seemed so many people were getting cancer. I was riveted.

She also told me the discouraging news that a doctor had missed the cancer two years before. The doctor had examined the lump in her breast, but had written it off as though it were nothing. That physician simply told her to keep a check on it. But time had gone by and this single mom of two wonderful children didn't have the lump checked until it had gone into the lymph nodes. She faced surgery, chemo, and radiation.

Some people can get away with a lumpectomy and don't have to get chemotherapy or radiation because the cancer has been caught so early. That wasn't true in Pat's case; for her it was going to be a much tougher battle, because the cancer had about two years to grow and invade the body. She also had a suspicious spot on her collarbone.

Pat stayed in constant prayer about this. People all over town were praying for her. Our family prayed earnestly for her. In other words, we call to God often on Pat's account. But with much prayer, surgery and treatment, we then got the word that the cancer couldn't be found in Pat's body! Praise God.

Pat did have to undergo eight chemotherapy treatments. Doctors planned to give her two treatments a week for four weeks. It was a Friday and the third day of her chemo. She was having trouble sleeping that night. So she dug out her Bible. It was a Bible she had carried with her since her teenage years. She read a little, and then tried to get some sleep.

Her prayer that night consisted of asking God for help and comfort through chemo and to use the chemo running through her body to kill the cancer. A couple of minutes after she closed her eyes, she felt a hard hit on her clavicle. She describes it as a quick jolt, like lightening. Her eyes popped open. She whispered, "God?"

About 30 seconds later, Pat felt the same type of jolt at the base of her neck. This time she said loudly, "God?

What is happening to my body? I know you are with me. Please comfort me." She says she felt God's presence but still felt fear and overwhelming excitement.

When she reached for her Bible (*The Living Bible*), she opened it to a page with her handwritten note: "My prayer." She had written the Scripture down as a teenager.

> *Lord, saving me will bring glory to your name. Bring me out of all this trouble because you are true to your promises. And, because you are loving and kind to me, cut off all my enemies and destroy those who are trying to harm me; for I am your servant.*
>
> —Psalm 143:11–12 (TLB)

She says she was led to read the next couple of verses.

> *Bless the Lord who is my immovable Rock. He gives me strength and skill in battle. He is always kind and loving to me; he is my fortress, my tower of strength and safety, my deliverer. He stands before me as a shield.*
>
> —Psalm 144:1–2 (TLB)

Pat said, "Brenda, I believe God healed me that night! It felt like an electrical charge." She went on to tell me that no cancer had been found at the base of her neck initially. But when she met with a doctor of radiology after that night, that doctor told her one of the first places her type of cancer metastasizes is to the base of the neck. She said her healing had been confirmed, and that she said she was given a miracle that night. "Brenda, I am humbled and honored that God has obviously chosen me for a special mission in life. He says in His Word that He has a plan for all of us. I pray every day that I will have sense enough to know what it is God wants me to do and to be brave enough to go forward and do it. I am truly blessed. God is back in my life and that is where He will stay."

I had also prayed for healing and one night felt an electrical charge go through my body. Being analytical, I asked doctors and nurses about it. They shrugged. Instead of immediately equating it with God's healing as Pat had, I looked for a logical answer to my own electrical surge. I was in awe of Pat's faith. She knew she was healed and that was the end of it.

In His Time

God's timing is amazing. Another story about healing by prayer came in the form of an email. I was checking emails from viewers when I came across one from a fellow cancer survivor, Lou Drummond. She had had a tough battle. Her cancer returned and doctors weren't hopeful. But she wrote: "Brenda, one night I was praying for healing and I felt this electrical surge and I knew in an instant what it was. I was healed."

Even though the cancer had traveled to other parts of her body, she believed in the gift of healing from the Lord.

Could it be? This story was too similar to Pat's and mine. While one had said she would continue with treatments because the Lord provides medicine for us, the other decided to cut the number of radiation treatments. But the fact remains all three of us had something happen during prayer. Lou's email read as follows:

Hello Brenda,

It's been a long time since I emailed you. Thought I would write you and give you an update. Wow, has it been a roller-coaster ride this last year. I ended up having two additional surgeries. The cancer had metastasized to many lymph nodes and my lung. The chemo my oncologist tried, which was about eight different ones, was not doing any good. The cancer kept spreading. The only thing left to do was to try a clinical trial. I prayed about it for a couple of days. The clinical trial they suggested I participate in was only in the first stage and had some severe side effects. I decided after much prayer, that I would go into the trial. My thinking was that just maybe, if the clinical trial did not help me that it would help someone else down the road.

I took three different chemos every week. It was

very difficult. I was in and out of the hospital a lot. I was so sick. But I would remind myself every day when I would just try and walk, that each step I took—I told the Lord—this step is for You and in Your name. I thought about Job. I typed up: GOD, I KNOW THAT YOU HAVE SHOWN ME FAVOR. I put that statement everywhere in my home as a reminder. I kept the thought in my mind all the time . . . that "[God] alone is my rock and my salvation, my fortress where I will never be shaken" (Psalm 62:2).

I haven't told many people this next part of what I did, but I wanted to share it with you for some reason. I would talk to my cancer. I would speak every day numerous times . . . that "you do not belong in my body . . . my body belongs to Christ and everything of Christ is good, not bad." I would command over and over through the name of Christ that it be removed from my body. I've always just talked to God like He was visible to me. By that I mean, if I couldn't find something I was looking for, I would say, "Lord, what did I do with such and such?" That may sound crazy to some people but I do know that He is with us all the time.

One day I was talking with God. I told Him that I was only a human and that I had my weaknesses, but I knew that He loved me. I told Him I knew there was something I was supposed to do, or I would not still be here in this world. I told Him that I was weak and to forgive me for my weaknesses. That moment, when I gave everything to Him . . . I felt His spirit from the top of my head to the tip of my toes. I knew that I was healed at that moment.

I asked for a CT scan the next chemo treatment. The CT scan confirmed I am cancer-free through the grace of God. Everyone in my oncology office was celebrating. I have grown very close to the chemo nurses. I have been able to witness to numerous people throughout my chemotherapy. The nurses have me talk with new patients. They tell me that I have been there so long that I am a fixture (lol). I still take weekly chemo, and my oncologist tells me that will be indefinitely. Some people tell me that I should stop chemo since the Lord healed me. I tell them that the Lord also gave me some common sense. It's not that I don't trust my Lord. I still have work to do. I have been praying so hard for the Lord to show me what I am to do with the rest of my life.

I had so much more happen that would take forever to tell you. But my answer with what I am supposed to do with my life . . . started with your email below. . . ."

—Lou Drummond

I was happy to encourage Lou about having faith in God and completely putting it in His hands. It was like seeing a baby bird learn to fly for the first time. I was so honored the Lord used me as a conduit for Him to work through her life. Now she's going on to help others. I had written to Lou Drummond about the Breast and Cervical Cancer Act of 2000 to help her to get treatments covered. But after going through the system, she found out a patient must find out about the cancer through their referral sources.

Now Lou Drummond is on a mission to help change that requirement through legal channels and help others cut through the red tape. I'm so proud of her. She is going to help many other cancer patients. Lou says God used me to touch her life, and now she's going on to touch many others. It's like the Lord's tapestry of life. It's wonderful to know we are a part of His plan.

Confidence in His Power

Then only days before turning in this manuscript, I was in the break room at the station, heating a cup of water for my afternoon green tea. Since cancer, everyday I have reached for a cup of green or black tea, which God has packed full of cancer-fighting nutrients. Another blessing is that God packed cancer-fighting nutrients into dark chocolate too!

In the break room was my six o'clock producer, Lisa Beasley. I asked her how her sister was doing. She'd been fighting breast cancer for a number of years. At last report the cancer was just about everywhere.

She said, "She's doing great!"

I was happy, surprised, and shocked. The last time I had asked about her sister's battle, the outcome did not look good; the breast cancer had returned for a third time, and she was going blind in one eye.

I said, "That's great, but wasn't she really sick?"

"Yes, but she believes the Lord healed her," she said with a big smile.

Susan Peterson, like me, is the mother of three boys. She had been a nurse and most recently had become a lawyer. Four years ago, when she was diagnosed, she was setting up a practice after being a stay-at-home mom for 11 years. She says through cancer she learned to lean more on her faith. Having a background in nursing helped her understand how serious her breast cancer diagnosis was. The cancer had advanced into two of her lymph nodes.

Susan had annual mammograms. In fact, she'd had one six months before she found a dimpling of one breast. She had leakage from her breast for some time, but doctors didn't diagnose it as cancer. She believes the cancer fell through the cracks especially since she had fibrocystic breasts. That is something I had before my double mastectomy; it's a condition that leaves the breast lumpy and bumpy. As a result, it's often harder to find cancer in women with this breast condition.

But when she went in to check out the dimpling, she was devastated by the news that she had cancer. It was a large tumor and the lymph nodes had been invaded. That meant the cancer had started moving through her body. She had a mastectomy, nine chemo treatments, and 47 radiation treatments. Then several months later, she opted to get the other side removed to cut down on her chances of a recurrence; she had another mastectomy and reconstructive surgery.

The next summer, she started to have muscle spasms in her neck. An MRI showed two vertebrae collapsed because of a tumor in her back. She had surgery the next day and started another round of radiation. She said doctors were not optimistic. Susan says she always prayed hopeful prayers for healing. But the day after that tumor was found, she started praying confident prayers.

When she returned home, four women showed up one day on her doorstep. One woman said to her, "We have good news for you. You are not going to die." They came to pray for her healing. Her mother and sister were there too. Until that day, she felt like she had a death sentence. One of the prayer warriors said, "We are here to share the news that God is a healer." Each woman had incredible stories of loved ones being healed. They, their pastor, and church prayed for Susan.

Later, Susan's brother continued to pray through Psalm 91 for Susan, which I also have marked in my Bible. This psalm had given me strength to know God would protect me. I chuckled when I saw the star next to it. The verse that helped Susan was also a word from God that helped me too!

One night, she had a dream and heard God say in a booming voice, "I'm setting you on a high place." She jerked awake because it seemed so real.

The next morning following cancer surgery, Susan was doing well. One week later, she went with some friends to church for prayer. The pastor didn't know Susan or that she was the person the doctors had not given hope. But when he made the call to pray for people, Susan went forward. He prayed. She says she immediately felt an electrical surge run through her body from the top of her head to the tip of her toes.

After that, she had bone scans. She was supposed to have cancer—otherwise known as a hot spot—on a vertebra, rib, and in her neck. She reports that after that prayer she had a scan and they were gone. But about a year later, yet another recurrence happened in her lower spine, liver, eye, and brain. A gamma knife operation cleaned the cancer from her brain and radiation was effective in stomping out the cancer on her optic nerve.

People from her church and all over town have committed to fast and pray for Susan daily. Places in her bones have been healing and spots on her liver shrinking. She's now regaining sight in her eye. She says, despite what all doctors predicted, she feels great! Daily,

Behind the Scenes of Breast Cancer

someone will lift her up and call and say, "I'm praying for you." Susan says she can feel people praying for her. Susan believes God is using prayer and her treatments and surgery to wipe away the cancer.

Our TV news station taped Susan's story and it flowed beautifully. It's not often that I don't have to prompt or ask questions of the interviewee. She was talking about her miracle as some people would talk about a wonderful vacation. The story aired on a Friday night. Monday when I got to my desk and opened my email, I had received a word of encouragement from a viewer about Susan's story. He wrote, "You may have given someone hope by airing this story."

The love of God can heal us here and in heaven. There is such awesome power that we cannot fully understand. The question is, *Why do some people get healed here on earth and others don't?* I asked Susan Peterson's pastor that very question. He's been in the ministry for 23 years. He's seen people healed miraculously after prayer and others who were not. He can't explain why and says we won't fully know why until we see the face of God in heaven.

> *Good people pass away; the godly often die before their time. But no one seems to care or wonder why. No one seems to understand that God is protecting them from the evil to come.*
>
> —Isaiah 57:1

Worship Study Questions

•Do I have faith that God is in complete control and can do anything?

_____

_____

_____

_____

•What in my life interferes with my time in His Word?

_____

_____

_____

_____

•What testimony can I share about God's supernatural power in my life?

_____

_____

_____

_____

_____

_____

Chapter Four

Rocks, Worms, Cheerios, and Trust

For anyone out there who doesn't know where you're going, anyone groping in the dark, Here's what: Trust in God. Lean on your God!
—Isaiah 50:10 (*The Message*)

"THAT'S ALL FOR NOW, and see you tonight at ten." I signed off the 6:00 P.M. news and dashed to the speaking event at a local Baptist church. There wouldn't be time for dinner with Doug and the boys. So I buckled into my small black car and reached for the baggy full of nuts I had packed earlier in preparation for this full night. As I munched and drove up the mountain to this women's gathering, I prayed the Lord would give me His words to speak. I carried my bag filled with rocks, Cheerios, and worm waste. Strange items for a church show-and-tell, but I had a plan.

I entered the room to the smell of chocolate and coffee and a view of hundreds of smiling faces. There were so many women going this way and that, sampling desserts, refilling coffee cups, and sharing stories with each other. It was a warm group. I could feel God's presence. Some of my running buddies were here as well as people I'd known through school functions or had met at the ballpark. Dear friends, casual acquaintances, and people I'd never met were all present. In a few moments I would reveal some of the most intimate details of my life and tell them all about my battle with breast cancer. Strange that the Lord would use me, one of the shyest people, to talk about body and soul. Here I was regularly talking to women about breasts and breast cancer.

There was Wanda McKoy, a pretty, sharp, blonde lady and a grandmother who didn't look like one. Whenever I saw her I would think *classy, Chanel, model.* She sat at the breast cancer awareness table with a bunch of items. A tireless worker for the Susan G. Komen Breast Cancer Foundation, Wanda often accompanied me to these speaking engagements to help get the word out about breast cancer; always ready to do whatever she could to help save another woman from the ravages of the disease to which she had lost her own mother as a child.

I really wanted to make this special, fresh, and pertinent to these women's lives. Some can relate to the cancer experience; for others, it's foreign. I know—at one time I never imagined I would have had cancer. I was always the healthy one in my family. I thought the Lord put me here to take care of everyone else. But on that day in February the doctor set me straight. I was indeed human and could get very sick. But how do you get the message across to someone who is the person I used to be—a person more concerned about today than eternity?

My days of floating freely around without any major disasters in my life ended the day the doctor said I had breast cancer. The only way for me to survive that crisis in my life was to hold onto the Lord Jesus Christ tighter than I ever had. I needed His strength and power to get through it. How could I make a room full of women understand that God is the only way to get through everything in life? That's right: rocks, worms, and Cheerios.

Rocks

I called on one older woman in the audience. "Say I give you a rock . . ." and I did. Then I gave the woman sitting next to her a bowl full of worm dirt. I gave the woman next to her a big box of Cheerios. "Which one has the most valuable gift?" I asked the group. "The simplest conclusion would be: the Cheerios. Ah, but you knew this was going to be a trick question. Imagine that grey lime rock in the palm of your hand. It's pretty boring to look at. Most women don't care much about rocks unless they are in jewelry.

"Now, children love rocks. They love to throw them, skip them on water, and just put them in their pockets to eventually end up in mom's dryer clanking around. But after a field trip to a rock quarry, I learned along with third graders that a rock is one of the most valuable things God has given us. I remember on the way to the rock quarry with several children in my car from the class, I hoped I could stay awake. But the field trip I thought would be the worst one ever, was actually the best one ever!

"That's where I learned that the grey lime rock is used not only to build roads and buildings, but it's also used for things like antacid, toothpaste, makeup, and minerals. Yes, that's right, makeup. From the largest boulders to the finest rock powder, God provided so much for us in just one rock. The company harvesting these treasures didn't waste anything. God's given us so much right under our feet. It's right in front of us and we often miss the blessings. Quite often it's easier to only see the rock and not all that's within the rock.

"I also learned that day that rocks hold treasures and clues to our history. They hold dinosaur fossils and plant fossils. A paleontologist was with us on the field trip to show the children some of the large dinosaur bones found after the rock was blasted by explosives. Instead of destroying the fossils, they allow fossil hunters to harvest them. During the field trip we were allowed to see treasures of the past. How wonderful God is to provide us with so much. Remember that rocks can also provide hours of entertainment for a child."

Worms

I continued, "Now you may wonder how worm waste can be a blessing. On another field trip to our local botanical gardens, I learned along with the children that worms eat garbage and turn it into rich soil. If it weren't for worms, that tomato you may have on your salad wouldn't provide you with much-needed nutrients. The little slimy creatures don't look pretty, but if they didn't exist, our horticultural system wouldn't work as well.

"Worms, by the way, are also being used in the battle against cancer. A University of Alabama at Birmingham researcher is involved in a study looking at the cells of worms to see how tumors are formed. Hopefully this research will lead to better understanding of what happens in the human body when tumors form, and ultimately lead to a cure for cancer. Did you ever imagine that worms were so important or valuable?

"God really has every detail handled. The more I learn about the world around us, the more I realize God has everything choreographed like a beautiful dance. He blesses us every day with things we don't even see or notice. What may seem insignificant really does have a purpose. If God has a purpose for rocks and worms, think about the purpose He has in our lives."

Cheerios

I asked my audience, "What do Cheerios have to do with all this? Cheerios provide clear blessings. But sometimes I

find myself pushing the biggest blessings away and interrupting God. I let fear, doubt, and my need to be in control
get in the way. Instead of trusting and letting the blessings
flow. Take my dog, Copper. He loves to eat. In fact, he'll eat
anything, anywhere, anytime. If he has a talent, I guess you
could call it eating. Every morning, he looks at me with his
big, brown, beagle eyes and begs for something delicious.
Cheerios are a staple at my house. So on a lot of mornings,
if there are not leftover eggs, Copper will receive the blessing of Cheerios.

"But what I notice, morning after morning, is that
Copper is pushing away the box as I'm pouring it out.
He pushes the source of the Cherios away from the bowl.
He does this so that he can get to the first pieces of cereal
poured out. But every morning I think, *If he'd just be patient
and sit back and wait until I'm finished pouring, he'd get a whole
lot more Cheerios.* But he gets a little greedy.

"I think that is how I am. Do I pounce on the blessings before I sit back, wait, and let God finish pouring
them out? During cancer, I had to slow down; I had to sit
back and wait. I had to watch others scurry around me
while I was in slow motion. While in pain and tired from
surgery, I took time to see the blessings. But now that life
has sped up again, I have to remind myself to slow down
and accept the blessings. There are so many blessings I get
too busy to see, such as the sunrise; the beauty of the day;
friendships; and simply sitting and sharing a meal with
my family. Those simple things are the biggest blessings.

"The new television, new car, new swimming pool, fancy vacation—they are all minor compared to the rich blessings our Father gives us each day. Sometimes we see them, sometimes we don't. I just imagine giving my children a truckload of presents and have them open them and not even notice or acknowledge the presents. Is that what we do? I think about the rocks and worms. It may sound funny thanking God for rocks and worms but they truly are gifts. But if God blesses us with rocks and worms, where else are there blessings we are not noticing? I'm also working on sitting back and letting God pour out the Cheerios without me interrupting Him.

"Through my cancer battle and beyond, when I trusted God, He provided absolutely everything I needed to get through the toughest time. Mainly, He provided the strength I asked for through prayer."

Immediate Results

I wondered and prayed that the crazy talk about rocks, worms, and Cheerios really got through. I hoped it really gave them something that would help them. After the speech, I greeted some of the women over by the table with the breast cancer fund-raising materials. Several women came up to me and said the speech helped encourage them. I praised God. But then something happened so that I knew the Lord had hit a home run. That night, He laid the rocks, worms, and Cheerios on my heart for a good reason.

A woman approached me explaining that she had been struggling with some things lately, and that her mother had died of breast cancer. Her mother had been a scientist who studied worms and their benefits to us. She knew that speech was a gift from God, reminding her that He could be trusted to handle whatever problem might come her way.

What a blessing to have the Lord deliver a specific message with clues like *worms* to touch a woman's heart. Even I had thought it was a little crazy to talk about worm waste, but I have no doubt the Holy Spirit used that reference to let her know He was ministering to her heart. God can be trusted. And she touched me because I have a special place in my heart for the children of breast cancer patients. I often say a special prayer for them, because one of my fears had been that my three little boys would be lacking something they needed and I couldn't provide it.

But the Lord provided so many people who delivered dinners, picked up the boys from school, and went to the grocery store to help out. He ministered to me inside and out. People prayed, called, offered support, and encouraged us. I thought I was part of a community but found out I was really part of a big family. The Lord showed me I had been blessed by His love and the knowledge that, if I would trust Him, I would never want for anything I need.

He also provided me the tools to get through tough times by trusting in His Word. The Bible holds answers for everything in life. Through prayer and Bible study, my doubts were answered time and time again. My prayer is: "Lord, help me to sit back and trust you more so that I can see Your blessings without rushing through life, trying to control everything and missing Your gifts each day!" Cancer helped me lean on and trust God; now I must remember the lesson and live a more fulfilling life thanks to Christ. "Not a single one of all the good promises the LORD had given to the family of Israel was left unfulfilled; everything he had spoken came true" (Joshua 21:45).

Do you ever feel like you're spinning your wheels in mud and, the harder you try, the deeper you get in the rut? Is that because you're trusting in yourself rather than trusting God? One recurring nightmare I had after cancer was that my car was stuck in the mud in a parking lot. I couldn't get it out. What was even worse than being stuck was the fact that I was ineffective. I was stuck! I wondered if the chemo dragging me down and tiring me out and the cancer-fighting drug I took daily that was sapping my strength had something to do with that.

One of my greatest fears is to be useless. I felt useless at times as a mother and a wife when I was too tired to do my duties. That memory of not being able to pick up my 18-month-old baby boy because of the surgery is probably one of the things that drives me today. I want to do it all and be there to live a perfect life. There it is—that word *perfect*! It is a word that can drive us all insane. The only thing perfect is God, His love for us, and what He provides for us. As much as we try to be perfect, we are still in the flesh. I'm humbled time and time again by that fact.

Most of my Christian friends always remind me to pray about everything in life. They are right. When I try to figure it out on my own, I inevitably mess it all up and get stuck in the mud, so to speak. But when I trust God with all my heart it all works! And just like Cheerios the blessings unfold and flow. The key is the heart. In the Bible, the Lord repeatedly tells us to believe and to trust Him with all our heart. When you pray, you should believe with all your heart that your prayer will be answered.

While sitting at my desk preparing for the 6:00 P.M. newscast, a coworker reminded me of the power of trusting God, "When you pray you have to believe with all your heart." We both searched the Bible trying to find the exact verse, but couldn't seem to put our fingers on it. A day passed and, no kidding, a friend emailed Mark 11:24: "I tell you, whatever you ask for in prayer, believe that you have received it, and it will be yours" (NIV).

For example, we had been talking about a recent family ski trip and the fact we had returned with no broken bones. We prayed no one would get hurt and we didn't. That may sound silly, but if you knew the five of us well, you would know there are many klutzy moments. So yes, returning from a ski trip with my husband's minor forehead abrasion *was* a miracle (we might have returned home with major breaks after all the falls). The other part of the miracle is that I was skiing with no ACL (anterior cruciate ligament) and no cartilage in my left knee. Remember, the ACL injury is the injury that puts many a football player on the shelf. With all the surgery I've had, it's one more I'm putting off until absolutely necessary.

My dear friend Sabrina Thomas recently reinvigorated my belief that we have to pray and believe with all our hearts. Her mother had previously endured two heart attacks and needed heart surgery. Days after surgery, she had a series of seizures and the doctor told the family she also had suffered a stroke. But this family has its prayer warriors; Sabrina said, since she had grown as a Christian, she wasn't begging God, she was trusting in His victory. The left side of her mother's body was supposed to be lifeless, but after significant prayer, her mother moved her leg and then her arm. An MRI showed no sign of a stroke! There was no brain damage.

Yet, the question Sabrina and I had was this: *If we had prayed the same way for our fathers, would they be alive today?* My belief is no. God has a time we are to be born and to die. I believe prayer can affect outcomes of health. But when we and our loved ones are taken home to heaven, this also is a victory. That's why we don't have to fear death. Yes, we miss our loved ones when they are gone from this earth, but we can know they truly are in a better place. As my seven-year-old reminds me, "It's a little greedy to want our Pap-pap to stay here sick when he can be healed in heaven." Cancer made me face the truth that we have a limited number of days on this earth.

I know there are times when I need to trust God more. I know if I trust Him to help me through the not-so-tough times as well as the times filled with crisis, I'll see more blessings. I know I've come a long way in trusting God and also know I need to trust him even more. After all, if I can trust Him to take care of the tiniest details with rocks, worms, and Cheerios, I can trust Him to take care of every aspect of my life.

Worship Study Questions

•Do I trust God?

_____

_____

_____

_____

•How can I begin to put more of my trust in Jesus?

_____

_____

_____

_____

•What do I need to put in His hands instead of my own?

_____

_____

_____

_____

Chapter Five

Give God the Glory!

My soul will boast in the Lord; let the afflicted hear and rejoice.

—Psalm 34:2 (NIV)

How fun it is to see my husband get excited when his favorite college team is on television. The Gators were about to play Ohio in the national championship. Doug's eyes were glued to the screen. The leftover twice-baked chicken sufficed for our football party. Even though we collectively gasped when Ohio State returned the opening game kickoff drive for a touchdown within seconds, the Gators responded with the next snap. The orange and blue dominated the game. The underdogs were top dogs in the end.

I stayed for a few minutes of the game because those dinner breaks from work don't last forever. But when I got home at about 11:00 P.M. after the late-evening news, Doug was listening intently to postgame interviews. The

Gators made a big statement by defeating Ohio. There on national television appeared Dallas Baker, the touchdown maker, being interviewed. He had taken off his helmet and jersey. Something was written on the front of Dallas Baker's shirt in marker: "I can do all things through Christ who strengthens me" (Philippians 4:13 NKJV). There he was, acknowledging God!

During the news, I sit next to a sports guy who quite often has stories about players who have been in trouble with the law. But looking at this acknowledgement of God was refreshing. In fact, Philippians 4:13 helped me through treatments, fatigue, and marathons when I felt like quitting. I'd say it to myself and sometimes aloud and I would find in that verse power to keep going.

Speaking of sports, it's easy to acknowledge our favorite sports teams, singers, actors, cars, and clothing designers. I notice that almost everywhere, you can find someone wearing their favorite beer on their T-shirt or a jacket. Beer and soda sellers seem to know how to advertise their products. I often wish I'd see as many Jesus commercials and shirts as I do ads for popular beverages. Think about it; what Jesus is offering—everlasting life in a glorious place—is free and priceless. A drink may last 30 minutes.

As a Christian, am I a very good public relations representative for my Lord? In the last five years, I've made many speeches acknowledging that God got me through a tough time with breast cancer. I know when I do acknowledge Him before a speech and ask Him to put in my mouth the words He wants me to speak, the speech goes very well. When I haven't said that prayer before a speech, it it didn't feel right, and the audience doesn't embrace the speech as well. I've written books and done radio interviews acknowledging God. But is there more I can do? Do I miss opportunities to give the Lord the credit?

Acknowledging God is simply putting Him first. I look at it this way: He's the Pilot and I'm the copilot. I'm here to serve Him. Somehow I feel like the word *acknowledge* takes all the pressure off of us. It reminds me it's up to God. In the five years after being diagnosed with cancer, my décor now includes crosses, and postings of Bible verses and the Ten Commandments. This helps me stay on track.

Another way I've grown spiritually since cancer is that I'm not afraid to pray in public. God is first in my life, and I'm not ashamed to acknowledge that. So as a family we pray at the local burger restaurant. Some people may disapprove. But one day after bowing our heads and praying together, a woman walked up to us and said she thought it was great that we prayed in public.

Why should it be common to pray at home, but the rules change if you're out to dinner? That short prayer in the day is a way to reconnect, thank Him, and acknowledge Him. It also is a break from the day-to-day stress of being a news anchor, wife, and mother. It reminds me that all the glory belongs to Him.

You may find it funny to know there are many

nights that, before I say good evening on the news before 175,000 people, I say, *Lord let this show be to your glory*. That's been a personal moment between God and me. But I share that with you to put perspective on a comment from a viewer.

While sitting at my desk one day, I received a call from a man who wanted to let me know that he appreciated my Christian attitude on the air. He said a child had been killed and a different news anchor in another state had reported that there was nothing to hope for now. The viewer said, "When you talk about a tragedy, whether you realize it or not, you always look for the hope. I can see that now and I thank you."

I was stunned. Did the Lord shine through? As a news person I'm supposed to be unbiased and give the facts so viewers can form their own opinions. I've tried to stick to that journalistic principal. Yet, without trying, people notice I have a hope that comes from the Lord. God uses His people and many times we may not even realize we're being used for His purposes.

Praise His Mighty Acts

By God's grace, He's allowed me to live. It's all about Him! I have a cross hanging in my bathroom where I can see it every morning. It reads: "By this all men will know that you are my disciples, if you love one another" (John 13:35 NIV). In the Bible verse before that, in which Jesus is talking and teaching His disciples during the last supper, He says, "A new command I give you: Love one another. As I have loved you, so you must love one another" (John 13:34 NIV). We can best acknowledge the Lord is living in our hearts and lives by loving others. What better way to tell the world that the Lord is in control? It's hard to love everyone all the time as we are commanded, apart from His help. This *is* one of the commandments: to love.

Love is the most important way to let the Lord's light shine through our lives. Since cancer, when I'm in a crowd, I look at all the differences in people and think that the Lord loves each one of them. Rich, poor, tall, short; I'm to love every one of them too! Can we love even if someone has road rage against us? That's what's commanded. I may not like the person's actions but I'm supposed to love him or her anyway. After all, Jesus loves me whether I'm at *my* best or not.

People often praise me because I look healthy, and I reply, "Praise Jesus." The Word says:

> *But as for me, I will always have hope; I will praise you more and more. My mouth will tell of your righteousness, of your salvation all day long, though I know not its measure. I will come and proclaim your mighty acts, O Sovereign LORD; I will proclaim your righteousness, yours alone.*
>
> —Psalm 71:14–16 (NIV)

I know it's only His grace that I'm here today. I want to acknowledge Him in all ways—He's the one who defeated cancer. The only reason I'm alive today is that the Lord still wants me on this earth. Perhaps He still has a lot of molding to do on yours truly.

When people comment about my bravery or state that I am such an inspiration, I hope each time I remember to acknowledge God. He is the one who held me up during a time I wanted to put my head in the sand like an ostrich. There's nothing amazing about me. What's amazing is God's love and power to be able to carry us through absolutely any situation. I give all credit to Him.

This verse gave me peace and helped me get through the fear during my diagnosis and treatment. It is still a power verse for me today, years after the cancer was removed from my body: "Trust in the LORD with all your heart and lean not on your own understanding; in all your ways acknowledge him, and he will make your paths straight" (Proverbs 3:5–6 NIV). The part that tells us to acknowledge Him in all ways speaks to me time and time again because once I was past the crisis, there was still the fear of the cancer returning. But one day in my bathroom, I had a serious talk with the Lord about this.

I was worrying about every bump and pimple. Finally I had to say, *Lord, You are in control, so I will hand all this worry over to You.* I can honestly say that took a weight off my shoulders. I couldn't live with the fear of cancer controlling me anymore. By acknowledging that

God is in control, I admitted I was weak and only He could take that burden off of me. *Trust* led me to give up the fear to Him. *Acknowledge* reminds me that no matter how many years I've lived beyond cancer, it's by His grace that I'm still here, not my doing.

Cancer surgery, hair loss, and weakness during chemotherapy were humbling. But acknowledging God has led to hope. The more I praise Him the more empowered I feel. "As for me, may I never boast about anything except the cross of our Lord Jesus Christ. Because of that cross, my interest in this world has been crucified, and the world's interest in me has also died" (Galatians 6:14).

It's All About Him

One of the more frightening moments after cancer came on a ski slope and was all about acknowledging God. You may wonder what a breast cancer survivor is thinking, flinging herself down a mountain! I wanted to see if I could. Before the trip, all that information about *lymphedema* kept haunting me. I was afraid, thinking, *What if I fall? Would the elevation be too high and cause my arm to swell? Would I hurt my knee that already has no anterior cruciate ligament and cartilage?* All part of the fear factor.

First of all, please don't be impressed with the fact I was skiing. During this ski trip to Utah with friends, I'm not sure that what I was doing down the smallest bunny hill could even be called real skiing. I'm the slowest and the most careful person ever to strap on skis. I'm sharing this to prove that when I'm in a crisis it's easy to acknowledge God. When I'm not in a crisis, I start to think I can do it on my own and forget to acknowledge Him. But just imagine holding onto the Lord each day in every way; how much richer our lives would be.

From the time I strapped on the boots that squeezed my shin like a vice, to the inability to maneuver once the skis were clamped onto the boots, I felt humbled. It reminded me how I was restricted and slowed down postoperatively. I was limited. But once I got on top of the bunny hill, all that restriction would be taken away by gravity and a lot of slick snow. A half-day lesson from a friendly grey-haired gentleman named George provided me with the tools to stop and slow down. *Lifesaving tools,* I thought. He was the only thing between me and a crash into a tree. I trusted George. He took pride in his students' progress and I didn't want to let him down. So I learned to snowplow, or turn the points of my skis inward as in the shape of a pizza. That fought gravity and slowed me down. Then we learned to lean forward to push down on the snow; that, too, provided some control.

Two-year-old children were learning the same lessons. Watching my own children progress on the bunny hill slope, I thought, *I'm a slow learner.* By midday in their ski school, they were learning to maneuver through an obstacle course. I was still working on the snowplow and hoping to enjoy a faster trip down the hill. My seven-year-old, Garrett, was fearless, his teacher reported. She said, "He's strong and determined." This came as no surprise. As the youngest, he's always trying to keep up with the big boys. Wow, she described him to a tee, on and off the slopes.

Garrett, Gabby, and Brooks all advanced quickly the next day to the more difficult slopes. But there I was clinging to the kiddy hill as some people call it. As I glided slowly back and forth downward, I noticed the snowboarders were on their knees more than they were up. I thought about how humbling this whole skiing experience can be. Like cancer, this was something that had to be conquered. I needed to let go and let God help me. But my own fears kept me from giving it all up and flying down the hill.

I kept saying to my kids and myself, *I have nothing to prove. I've already fought my battles and I just want to have fun.* But it wasn't as much fun knowing the rest of the family was somewhere else on the mountain and there I was still doing skiing 101. I heard my friend's words ringing in my head, "You'll have to get away from that!" I thought, *Why can't I just stay in this safe place and stay stagnant? I should be able to keep my role as bunny hill ambassador; I enjoy meeting new people as they pass through the beginners' lift.* But that's not how God made me. I had to move up to the next slope and I knew I had to try.

Love Lifted Me

So there I was, on the next lift with my husband and seven-year-old son. It was a faster lift that went much higher than the kiddy lift I had come to call home. With each yard, as we rose higher in altitude, I felt my blood pressure rise too! I could hear my heart pounding in my chest. I remembered my fear of heights. This was a bad time to recall such a thing. But there I was praying as the lift took us to a new height. I asked if they were sure this wasn't Mount Everest. With every low whimper I made as we got close to shooting off the lift, my seven-year-old was snickering. *Lord, please help me,* I said silently. *I know You will help me do this. After all, You got me through cancer.*

A few minutes later, there we were at the top of a mountain. It didn't seem so bad until we started to descend. Garrett wanted to get to the bottom as fast as possible. I, on the other hand, wanted to get there as slowly as possible.

Doug looked bigger and stronger somehow in his ski bibs and puffy winter jacket. He said, "Follow me," and told Garrett to wait for us. Of course my little guy in the bright orange jacket only has one speed and that's fast. So the orange blur was past us and disappeared. About that time the slope seemed to drop like the side of a box —straight down. That's when I started acknowledging God out loud and praying, *Sweet Jesus, help me!* I fell, I got up, and yes, He did help me get off that mountain.

Cancer was like a slippery slope. I didn't know what was around the corner and I didn't know when life was going to drop off. I had to acknowledge the fact that only the Lord is the One calling the shots.

The mere fact that a cancer survivor was on the slopes was a feat. I recalled all the people after surgery saying what I couldn't do and what I shouldn't do and that I had to protect the arm without lymph nodes. Some health experts disagree on how to prevent the arm from swelling because the lymphatic flow under the skin has been compromised by removing lymph nodes. Those little sacs are put in place by God to catch sickness. When cancer tries to progress through the body it travels through and invades lymph nodes. Even though I wasn't up on the mountain summit, *skiing* was a victory.

The whole lymph node situation can be scary. The fact that I know there is a possibility cancer could pop up in my body can be scary. But I'm not giving those things power in my life by acknowledging them. I won't allow cancer or its threat to rule my life. I will acknowledge that the Lord Jesus Christ is in control and is the focus of my life. This brings me peace.

From skiing to cancer and everyday life, I'm trying to acknowledge Him more than ever now. The more I do, the more secure I feel. My Father loves me and is in control of my life. I don't have to worry about the turns, the drop-offs, or the trees as long as He is guiding me and carrying me through.

Worship Study Questions

•How can I better acknowledge God?

_____

_____

_____

_____

•How does it make me feel to acknowledge God?

_____

_____

_____

_____

•What changes do I need to make in my life, in order to acknowledge Him better?

_____

_____

_____

_____

Chapter Six

Running the Race

By day the LORD went ahead of them in a pillar of cloud to guide them on their way and by night in a pillar of fire to give them light, so that they could travel by day or night. Neither the pillar of cloud by day nor the pillar of fire by night left its place in front of the people.

—Exodus 13:21–22 (NIV)

IT WAS THE NIGHT BEFORE my second marathon. And as all marathoners will tell you, except for probably the elite runners, I had my doubts. I'd trained for months and many miles. I ran the 20-mile training run and even added a mile and a half that day for good measure, to give myself that extra confidence. Running had become therapy after cancer. It was a way to clear my head and made me feel I was even clearing my body of toxins. On days I ran alone, I talked to God and, more importantly, listened to Him. Usually running was relaxing and was a time to relieve the stresses of being a cancer survivor.

But on the eve of the 26.2-mile run, the thought of running made me panic. I was breaking out in a sweat. *Can I do this? Am I crazy? Everyone who is not a runner says I am. Will I fall and break something? Will my heart give out? What if I pass out and let down all those people fighting cancer? I made a big deal about the training on the news. Will I have to go on camera and admit to 175,000 that I DNF'd? That's what is next to the names of people who did not finish the marathon. Oh no if I could just take this commitment back!* I said to my oldest son, nine years old at the time: "Brooks, I don't think I can do this thing."

"Huh? What?" he said.

Brooks, being the oldest, became my sounding board. I had rustled him out of deep concentration from his video game.

I said, "I don't think I'm going to do this marathon tomorrow . . . I don't think I can. I should take my temperature. I bet I'm sick and that's it. I cannot do this marathon. What was I thinking, Brooks?!"

I don't know what I expected of this child. I certainly didn't expect wisdom and encouragement on the level I received from him. It was as though God were delivering a message to me through the mouth of a "babe"?

Brooks looked at me and said, "Mom!" In a fatherly tone, he continued, "Come look at this."

He pointed to the marathon medals Doug and I had earned the year before. Doug had thoughtfully mounted and framed our medals and our pictures together. Obediently, as if I was the child and he was the adult, I read the word he was pointing to on the back of the medal. "It says FINISHER!"

"Mom, that's what you are. You are a finisher! You did it last year and you'll do it again this year!" Brooks said.

I looked at him with tears welling up in my eyes and I asked, "How did you get so wise?"

"It's just what you would have told *me*, Mom!

Clutching Bible verses and running with my friend Gwen Pierce, we recited the Bible verses again as we needed to pull strength from them. Brooks was right: we crossed the finish line! "I can do all things through Christ who strengthens me" (Philippians 4:13 NKJV). "For you have rescued me from death; you have kept my feet from slipping. So now I can walk in your presence, O God, in your life-giving light" (Psalm 56:13).

Was it arduous? Yes. But somehow the Lord allowed me to put one foot in front of the other, and through His strength, we finished the race. It was a privilege and blessing to be healthy enough to finish 26.2 miles! I have no doubt the Lord wanted us to finish the marathon. I prayed for it not to glorify us, but Him.

Through five and a half marathons, the Lord has made my path straight. He guided me and kept me going when I was at my weakest point. A marathon is a lot like life with cancer: you need endurance, perseverance, and hope that you will finish the race. Without that hope, I'd be sitting on a curb on the side of the road. In life, isn't that what it means to lose hope? We give up. But in God's Word, He promises us a future. He tells us to hope in the Lord. Giving up doesn't get you anywhere but miserable.

I can remember when I felt like giving up. There were times after surgery when it was so hard to get out of bed simply to go to the bathroom. But the Lord kept lifting me out of bed through the people who loved me. God showed me my blessings were greater than my losses. I'd look at my sweet husband and three little boys and know I had to get up, as not to let them down.

The Lord helped lead me through much prayer. In my bathroom after surgery, fighting and suffering with the side effects of surgery, I asked God, *OK, what now Lord? You'll have to show me who I am. I don't know how to go on by myself.* After crawling back in bed, my four-year-old son Gabby said, Mommy, I feel God's arms around us right now." He delivered the message that God was holding me. I felt it, too, when he said it.

God's Timing

It's hard to understand even after much prayer why some lose their battles with cancer, and others survive. But the truth is that we are all here for a relatively short time. Even a hundred years is a blink of an eye. I'll never forget the week I was running and praying specifically that we would have a closer walk with the Lord. You may recall in my first book, I prayed for God to reveal my mission in life. Oh, He did! One month after that prayer, I found a lump in my right breast that turned out to be cancer. My mission was clearly to warn others about cancer, but more importantly to offer them the hope I found in salvation through the Lord Jesus Christ.

A few days after this more recent request for a closer walk with the Lord, I had my answer with a phone call from my husband. "Hey Bren, can I tell you something?" I could hear the stress in the strained sound of his voice and knew instantly something wasn't right.

"I'm not working at the radio station anymore. I just found out!"

Well, there's that horse-kicking-me-in-the-gut feeling. I wished I were right there next to him to take him in my arms and tell him it would be OK. I couldn't do that, so I prayed for the right words to say. "It's going to be OK; it's not a life-threatening illness. We'll get through this."

And we did—even though Doug had this afternoon radio talk show gig evaporate, he still had work as the studio host for the Big 12 basketball show with ESPN for part of the year. But the local connection to sports and sports fans was nice. He was the best sports-talk host in the region. But the station decided going all-political was their new tack, though some questioned the move. Yet, once again, God used this life change to work His goodness. Without that life altering experience, we wouldn't have grown into new and different opportunities that have been a blessing. "All things work together for good to those who love God, to those who are the called according to His purpose" (Romans 8:28 NKJV).

We asked God to show us the way, to give us something to hold onto. It felt as though we were swimming in the dark, in a murky lake on a foggy day, and couldn't see the other side. I knew God was there but I couldn't see where this would all end up. Doug and I knew it would give us a closer walk with Him. It's funny how life's little crises will do that for you. There we were holding onto our Father's hand a little tighter and praying more earnestly. "Let my prayer be set forth as incense before You, the lifting up of my hands as the evening sacrifice" (Psalm 141:2 AMP).

One day after much prayer, I looked at the clock radio in my bathroom while getting ready to head to the television station for the evening shift. I thought, *How strange . . . the numbers are distorted in a way that I've never seen before. The numbers were 25:21.* Keep in mind, that's never happened before or in the years since. But I had been looking for a confirmation that everything was going to be OK. I just wanted Doug to be happy with his position in life. I wanted us to be OK as a family. I was doing my part and budgeting at the grocery store. *That doesn't make any sense,* I thought. I shrugged and moved on.

I put the clock malfunction out of my head. I jumped in my car and headed to work, continuing to pray for Doug and for guidance, and there on the license plate in front of me were the same numbers I had seen on my clock radio. And "Matthew" was attached to these numbers. God didn't speak that day . . . He shouted! I called Doug and said, "I know it's going to be OK. I think you will be doing a lot of things! Not just a radio gig!" God reassured us through the Bible verse that read: "His master replied, 'Well done, good and faithful servant! You have been faithful with a few things; I will put you in charge of many things. Come and share your master's happiness!'" (Matthew 25:21 NIV).

And that's exactly what came to pass. Doug is now working with the PGA on XM Radio, ESPN, running his own company, Doug Bell Communications, and more! His business has flourished. He has what many men refer to as a dream job. He gets to cover sports all over the country including stars like Tiger Woods and Phil Mickelson at the Medina Country Club. This has been an unusual blessing. But the Lord is always reminding us He is in control of our days. "You can pray for anything, and if you believe that you've received it, it will be yours" (Mark 11:24). "So encourage each other and build each other up" (1 Thessalonians 5:11).

God has a plan and a *time* for everything in our lives. Sometimes months or years after a crisis, I can see how God used it for good. I know if I depend fully on God instead of myself, He will show me where I'm supposed to go and what I am supposed to do.

I was in a six-mile race through the streets of down-town Birmingham, and within two miles of the finish line, a tall man with dark hair ran and kept pace with me. He recognized me as the local news anchor even through my sweat. As we ran along, he said, "See that hospital up there; you have power to help others defeat cancer. When people go in there, they are scared. By Jesus's stripes you were healed; now you have the power to help defeat cancer and especially the *fear* of cancer. You can go to pray with those people and help them. You've been given power by the blood of the lamb that healed you!"

If I ever stop to wonder what my purpose is in life, which path I should travel, I remember that I'm here to help others, pray with them, and help them draw closer to the Lord. From answering emails and phone calls for people who have been newly diagnosed or simply sitting there and looking healthy after a cancer battle for those who are going through it, I'm honored to be the Lord's servant. There is no greater feeling than to know I've helped take some of the sting of fear away for some of my sisters and brothers in the fight. There is no greater joy than to know I can serve the Lord.

I believe the Lord will make your path straight, too, if you ask Him to guide you as you run your "race." The Lord has a purpose for all of us. He led the Israelites with a cloud of dust in the day in the desert and a col-umn of light at night. He parted the Red Sea. He'll make our paths straight too!

Worship Study Questions

•What path in my life have I been uncertain about?

_____

_____

_____

_____

•What should I ask for when I pray about where I'm heading spiritually?

_____

_____

_____

_____

•Where do I think the Lord is leading me?

_____

_____

_____

_____

•What crisis in my life can I use; to learn from, to serve others, and to glorify Christ as I run this race called life?

_____

_____

_____

_____

Chapter Seven

Defeating Fear and Worry

Can all your worries add a single moment to your life?

—Matthew 6:27

I CRIED THROUGHOUT THE MOVIE *The Passion* during the scenes where Jesus was depicted beaten and persecuted for us. But it was that enactment of what He said to His mother that still rings in my ears: "Mother, I will make everything new again." On this earth, everything wears, decays, crumbles away, and perishes, and there seems to be so much to fear in this world: fear of heartbreak, fear of getting sick, hurting, losing our livelihoods, and fear of death. But Christ died on the cross for us to defeat all fear in our lives and to give us new lives. When I choose to reach up for His hand and give Him my burdens, He will take them and carry me through the storms of life.

In fact, a storm reminded me that things on this earth are very fragile and temporary. During the night, two huge tree limbs crashed onto our two cars parked in our driveway. Yes, in an instant, the cars we depend on, houses we take shelter in, and relationships we count on can crumble under the pressures of this world. But the one true source I can count on is my Rock, the Lord Jesus Christ. His love never changes. He is stronger than anything of this world.

Time also has a way of eating away at the things of this world. After insurance adjusters did their work about a week later, Doug and I were returning from dropping off one of the cars for repairs. We chatted about how the kids had grown and about an old picture we'd seen the day before.

Doug said, "Isn't it amazing how time has flown? I feel like I was just holding that baby and now he's so tall!" In fact, Brooks is very proud of the fact that he has me by four inches as a teen now. Time does fly. It doesn't seem that long ago when *I* was going back to school.

I remember the fear I felt each year about going back to school when I was a little girl. The new clothes my mother bought me felt a lot like new armor. It was one way to help me feel like I was prepared and ready for the school year ahead. But even that new plaid dress and shiny new shoes didn't wipe away the fear of possibly getting a mean teacher or a class with the worst bully in school.

While I worried about getting an ogre for a teacher, thankfully she or he always turned out to be one of the kindest people. I look back at how I lost sleep over something that never happened. My stomach hurt and I went down a list of what-ifs that never happened. You would think after 12 years of that night-before-school fear, I'd learn not to worry. I didn't learn not to worry until I actually had a lot to worry about years later, as a grown woman.

My cancer diagnosis was so overwhelming. I literally was shaking when the doctor was telling me I had a deadly disease. First there was a fear of dying. Then there was the fear of the pain and the fear of losing the people I loved because I thought my body would be mutilated by cancer and surgery. My fear was exhausting. I finally had to come to the point where I was so wearied by fear that I had to pray and ask the Lord to take it all from me. He did carry the burden. Almost instantly after saying that prayer, I felt the heavy weight of fear and worry lift. Worry is a horrid state.

Even as a child, when I was in first grade, Mrs. Conley, whom I loved dearly, lovingly nicknamed me her "little worrywart." Coming from her, that nickname always made me chuckle inside and realize how silly it was to worry about nothing. She was an incredible teacher and leader in my life. I was painfully shy. I was terrified if an adult would even talk to me. I think to this day that if it weren't for Mrs. Conley, I would not be a TV news anchor.

I also think how God has a sense of humor. How funny it is that a little girl from a steel town, who was so afraid to talk to anyone—no less a crowd—would talk to more than one hundred thousand people every night. And I was shy about my body and now I regularly talk about breasts and breast cancer to groups of people throughout the state. It's only God who can take our weaknesses and shine by making us strong through those weaknesses. I'm learning fear is destructive; trusting God is not.

Back to School

Recently, on back to school night, a pretty mother with long blonde hair and a face that could grace any fashion magazine said to me, "We have something in common." When I heard those words, I knew it wasn't just that our two sons shared the same teacher this year. She said she'd had cancer but it wasn't breast cancer; it was skin cancer. She'd had a year of hard treatments. It's amazing how cancer survivors can have such an intimate conversation in a room full of parents *oohing* and *ahhing* over the classroom and their children's biographical sheets. The connection between cancer survivors is so strong. I wanted to buy her a cup of coffee, sit down, and chat. It turns out she was dealing with some percentages that put me to shame.

At the time I was waiting for a pathologist to release some test results on my five-year-old tumor.

The results had been held hostage until the patholo-gist's office was guaranteed payment from my insur-ance company. However, this woman was dealing with more than a 90 percent recurrence rate the first year and, in her second year, was almost celebrating with a recurrence rate above 60 percent.

The percentage numbers were much lower for my cancer. I was in the 15 percent recurrence range. We had much different chances given human doctors. But we both put our fears in God's hands. We both surrendered to God, allowing Him to handle the fear. I'd like to wipe away that sting of fear for others. There's nothing worse than first hearing the diagnosis. I had to turn it over to the Lord and say, *"Lord, I can't handle this so I'm putting it in your hands, so please handle it for me."*

I also feel the responsibility to make a difference. I personally think nothing short of me finding a cure for cancer would suffice. That's why I get so excited about doing stories on cancer researchers looking for the cure. But then I realize that the good Lord has every day of our lives planned out, and when He plans to call us home, that's when we'll go. All the doctors' statistical information and hypotheses won't change God's plan.

There's so much to be fearful about in this life. Fear of failure is one of my top ten. I want to do everything to the best of my ability. That fact drives me a little crazy at times because I do so many different things. Sometimes

I feel like I'm in the middle of a rob-Peter-to-pay-Paul dilemma. Time is certainly the most precious thing of all, and I constantly try to jam as much into my time as possible. Is it a side effect of being a cancer survivor? Partly. But I've always been an overachiever. I want to see the sun rise, the sun set, I want to be at every school function and do the story to remember at work, have meaningful family time, and make my seven-year-old's king outfit for the school play. I'd be happy to make the cupcakes for the party afterwards too!

My fear of failure drives me to get too little sleep and go, go, go. You may ask, "What is she doing writing a book and a DVD project? I've asked myself all that too. I feel the reason is that the good Lord kept me here for a purpose after my cancer diagnosis and He wants me to share His hope. Do I feel challenged and stretched at times? You betcha. Am I still here to fulfill the Lord's purpose? Yes. He gives me strength and encouragement when I'm least expecting it.

I fear failing as a mother. Sometimes it feels like a slippery slope. When they don't obey, I worry. It's that fear that separates me from the blessings God has for me daily and moment by moment.

I learned that lesson during my cancer treatments. It's a lesson I need to remember. How many days, weeks, or even years do we worry about something we have no control over? It might not even happen, but we've wasted so many days worrying. The Lord told us that we add nothing to our lives because of worry (Matthew 6:27).

Since cancer, big things don't worry me as much as the little things. I know God will handle the big stuff. He already has in helping me through cancer. It's the little things in life that are easier to get caught worrying about. I figure since I survived to be a mother, I should do my best. But sometimes it seems there aren't enough hours in the day to bake cookies with the kids, and sit and enjoy a good book with them, like I think I should. There's always a practice we have to run to or a mandatory activity.

I'd like to start a movement to simplify life, to add more precious time with my family. But as a country song blares out on the radio, it seems like the world keeps spinning faster, and I'm just trying to keep up.

Why am I here? The Lord has shared in my heart that I'm supposed to encourage and be a partner to my husband, encourage and guide my four boys along this path of life, and encourage others. I believe my children will have big missions from God one day. I've been appointed to help the Lord shape these fine young men. If I let fear control me, I'm not efficiently helping the Lord.

What is it you fear the most? If you're reading this book, cancer may be one of your top ten. Or perhaps it's the fear of a recurrence that gives you that funny feeling in your stomach. This verse helped me during my battle. The Lord spoke to me to give me confidence in Him: "He will renew your life and sustain you in your old age" (Ruth 4:15 NIV).

Doug had to remind me again, "Isn't it strange that life goes by so fast, and then all of a sudden you are in your eighties, and then you die?"

"Yes, but we know it doesn't end there. It would be tragic if life ended with old age. But thanks to the love of the Lord Jesus Christ and His willingness to die for our sins, life does not end at 80, 90, or even 100." Because of the love of Christ, we have a promise of a future with Him. He does make everything new again if we accept this.

I remember when I feared getting old. However, it's one of my life goals now! My dream is to walk on a beach hand in hand with my husband during our golden years. I also want to be the best grandmother ever. I want to bake homemade cookies and spoil the little tykes. Cancer helped me see the blessing of getting old. God encourages me: "Don't be afraid. Just stand still and watch the LORD rescue you today" (Exodus 14:13).

Hope in Christ

Doug had returned from work in Youngstown, Ohio, recently and we went to the local mall for two of the boys to play the piano for shoppers. Later that evening, we were planning to listen to the Christmas Trio, a singing group made up of three special men from Alabama.

One happened to be a first baseman for the New York Yankees, Andy Phillips. I had heard about the trio while listening to the "Rick and Bubba" morning radio show. The baseball player had touched my heart. He had talked about how we are to find joy in this life and not be so hard on ourselves. I thought to myself, *Wow, what good Christian inspiration for the boys, to be the best you can be for the Lord.* I knew the boys would get a kick out of it.

Well, there we were, on time! That, I thought, was a miracle in itself for us. We got there a few minutes before the program started. I thought, *This is what it's like to be on time.* The music introduction DVD started and included three incredible men. One sporting a New York Yankees uniform on the video, smashing a home run! *This is great!* I thought! Then they appeared on stage in their suits. They were beaming with joy and love. These *men are great representatives of the Lord,* I thought.

Then when they opened their mouths to sing, it was one of the most moving moments of my life. These manly men were singing with such sweet praise about the tiny baby Jesus. I wanted to fall to my knees! Song after song, they endeared themselves to me and, looking at my boys and Doug, they were impressed too! And just as Doug had predicted, in the middle they gave the all call for unbelievers to come forward. But before the last song, the baseball player Andy Phillips gave his testimony. The Scripture that comes to mind that explains the gist of what he said is this: "Even though I walk through the valley of the shadow of death, I will fear no evil, for you are with me" (Psalm 23:4 NIV).

It was wondrous. But then he shared about his wife who had lost a baby and that she'd discovered she had cancer. He said so far the treatments hadn't gone as well as he'd hoped. The tears were pouring down my face. *Had the Lord led me here tonight?* The connection was so strong. I was drawn to this young family. I wanted to reach out. I thought I'd come to listen to a few "Hallelujahs!" and "Praise God's" and be on our way to tuck in the boys.

But no—this was a deep, meaningful, spiritual moment. This precious man talked with such love about his wife. He talked about the hope for a family being dashed and the added blow of his wife's cancer. Then he talked about how he had hope. He had hope because of his faith in the Lord Jesus Christ! Here he was a big baseball player on the top of the world and he said how he and so many others with nothing had so much in common. The baseball didn't matter; or the uniform. He was reduced to a place where only God could help.

I completely understood. People, who endure cancer, experience the fact that all this could end in an instant. In fact, he talked about his friend Cory Lidle. A week before he crashed into a building in New York with his plane. Lidle had spoken about the fact that he had a parachute and he could jump out in the event of a crash and save himself.

How often do we have a plan? But our plans and we ourselves aren't big enough to cover it all. Face it; we need God to cover it all. We are mortal. We can die at any moment. Life, as I learned through cancer, is very fragile. Even if we have a parachute plan, we may never get to access it. God is the only way—the only way to have true hope. This young first baseman knows that no matter how scary life gets, with faith everything will be alright in the end. Thank You, Lord, for reminding me that all the frustrations of life really don't matter. It's Your love and loving and caring for others that really matters.

Andy Phillips defeated fear with the hope and faith he has in the Lord Jesus Christ. Can we all have that kind of hope and faith? You betcha. First pray for it. The Lord delivers; lay your heavy burdens on him. "You are a shield around me, O LORD; you bestow glory on me and lift up my head" (Psalm 3:3 NIV).

Fear can come during illness or from a threat from another human being. Recently I had a situation with a suspected would-be stalker, who had delivered a letter. But I immediately prayed about it, and realized that the devil wants us to live in fear. That separates us from God's power. God says, "I am with you, and no one will attack and harm you . . ." (Acts 18:10).

If we are focusing on fear, we are not moving forward praying and focusing on His awesome power. So I made a decision. I would not live in fear. The Bible contains verses such as "don't be afraid" and "God has not given us a spirit of fear" (Isaiah 41:10; 2 Timothy 1:7). The Lord carried me through cancer; I know He has legions of angels to surround and protect me. I can rest in knowing that. "The LORD will be your everlasting light. Your days of mourning will come to an end" (Isaiah 60:20).

God is serious about us trusting Him. It's almost like being on a rope bridge over a volcano. If you focus on getting to the other side instead of looking down into your ultimate destruction, you'll get to the other side unharmed. That's what God wants for you. He wants to get you to Himself without harming you. "Don't be afraid! Don't be discouraged!" (Deuteronomy 1:21). We can defeat fear of cancer, failing, and harm from other human beings, if we simply hold our Father's hand and let Him handle it all.

Lord, I want that assurance that You promise in Your Word—that I have nothing to fear.

Suddenly, Jesus was standing there among them! "Peace be with you," he said. As he spoke, he showed them the wounds in his hands and his side. They were filled with joy when they saw the Lord!
—John 20:19–20

Worship Study Questions

•What do I fear most?

_____

_____

_____

•Is that fear getting in the way of my relationship with God? How?

_____

_____

_____

_____

•What's my prayer for defeating fear and living in God's glory?

_____

_____

_____

_____

•Am I too busy to recognize the answers and miracles in my own life?

_____

_____

_____

_____

Chapter Eight

Between Two Worlds

This is the message we have heard from him and declare to you: God is light; in him there is no darkness at all. If we claim to have fellowship with him yet walk in the darkness, we lie and do not live by the truth. But if we walk in the light, as he is in the light, we have fellowship with one another, and the blood of Jesus, his Son, purifies us from all sin.

—1 John 1:5–7 (NIV)

"NO, YOU MAY NOT have any more candy! You've had enough! No you can't have an Icee either," a mother said in a firm and loud voice.

"Heads u-u-u-up," the crowd of little league parents, grandparents, and siblings yelled in unison.

The smell of the ballpark dirt coupled with the

smell of French fries, hot dogs, and chicken fingers, and sweaty little boys is the best smell on earth to me. How so many adults can be reduced to children, reliving their glory years while yelling at their kids to get a hit and catch balls, is amazing. The warm late spring sun on the backs of the fanatic fans isn't the only thing to get them hot under the collar.

"You're out!" yells the umpire.

A gasp in unison from the Oriole parents is followed by the sounds of disbelief. "Huh? Wha'? You're kidding?! No way!"

A teenager, who played at the park a few years before, is now the umpire. This is a kid who hasn't quite grown into his big feet yet, is making manly calls and is the judge and jury on this ball field. He's trying his best to make the right calls. Let's face it, there isn't a human alive that can see every move on every base at the same time. But he maintains umpire dignity while shaking in his shoes because some of the parents start to sound like bullhorns.

Why is it that true personalities come out in the adults during their kids' little league games? Me included: I have to suppress the type-A tendency to rip the umpire and yell, "Crush the competition!" The funny thing is that today we're arch opponents with the other team. Tomorrow or next season, we're playing on the same side. The perspective shifts.

With three boys playing ball, I've come to love the

cloud of dust kicked up by the runner sliding into home. The camaraderie isn't bad either. People who were total strangers the month before now cheered for my son, "C'mon Gabby, you're the man!"

He did well during the regular season and my high achiever was determined to be an all-star and play on the team after the season ended. This extra long season is for the children, and especially parents, who just didn't get enough of the screaming, yelling, and competition in the spring season.

I love the ballpark and all it represents: youth, hope, achievement, growth, and baseball! But sometimes I feel like I'm caught between here and there, between two worlds. I wanted to stay here on this earth to raise my boys but I surrendered to God five years ago and my perspective shifted. I began to see life in a different light. As the writer of Ecclesiastes attests, much of "this" doesn't matter. Some of the stuff that we get hot under the collar over simply doesn't matter. What matters ultimately is our relationship with God.

Arguments with referees come and go. Who wins and who loses doesn't really matter. It's the kids who learn how to lose at the local ballpark who gain the most in life. Let's face it. If we were only here to win and prove who is the biggest and strongest of them all, that would be a pitiful existence.

Sometimes when people get upset about events at work or on the road, or engage in trivial tiffs, I feel that tension between this world and the next. I want to shout, *None of that stuff matters! Get it straight and listen to your God. He has wonderful, miraculous plans for you! He did in my life and He does in yours!* Surviving cancer opened up a whole new world of understanding what *does* matter.

Being very ill and lying in a hospital bed with a deadly condition is scary but we learn ultimately we're in God's hands. Why does God allow pain and heart-ache? Whew, that's a question with which many of us struggle. But the truth is, the Lord is glorified the most during our hardest moments in life. The more we lean on Him during those tough times, the more we can see Him working.

These bodies we are given do wear out. The one thing that we can count on even when our body fails is that God gives us a promise of hope and a future. "For I know the plans I have for you,' declares the LORD, 'plans to prosper you and not to harm you, plans to give you hope and a future'" (Jeremiah 29:11 NIV).

Life and New Life

That future isn't here on this earth in these bodies; He promises a future in heaven, a real place, a different world. I'll share an experience I had which I believe is assurance that life goes on even when our bodies give out. God reaffirmed this truth to me in March 2005, when my father was about to turn 84 years old.

You'd never know it by looking at him. He looked decades younger because he loved to work vigorously (which is how I inherited my energy, as my mother often reminds me). My sister Linda and I decided we needed to clear our busy schedules and make arrangements to surprise Dad for his birthday. We knew there might not be that many more to celebrate with him. He was spry, with the exception of a few moments when a heart valve would close and he would pause and have trouble breathing. He'd pop a nitroglycerin pill, wince at the bitter taste, and go on.

Linda and I decided not to let Mom in on the plan because we knew she would push herself to get the house ready. By the time we arrived, *her* heart would be aching from the Marine-style, swab-the-deck operation she would undertake. Linda and I kept our dad-visit covert. We didn't tell anyone we were coming.

Linda flew from south Florida and I flew from Birmingham into Charlotte, North Carolina, where we met and flew on to Philadelphia. Feeling like a kid about to be in trouble with the folks, I dialed the phone from the airport. "Hello, Mom?" How are you?"

"I'm having trouble hearing you; are you at a basketball game with the kids?"

Linda waived her hand at me, "Go on, tell her."

"Well . . . Mom, I have something to tell you. We are at the Philadelphia airport."

"Whaaaaaaaaaaaaaaaat?" My mother said in

high-pitched shock. "What on earth are you doing there?"

"We are going to surprise Dad for his birthday. We just thought we'd call ahead so he wouldn't be too shocked. We didn't want to give him a heart problem."

"I have nothing washed! You stinker!"

An hour later, we were sitting at the dining room table in the house that my parents called home for the past 45 years. We talked, chatted, and for the first time in my life, my dad was speechless at the gift of time we had given him with his family united in honor of him.

Later that night after dinner, my dad brought me something that he held as one of the biggest treasures in his life. Sheepishly he said, "Maybe you might want to hold onto this one day...."

"What, Dad?" I asked.

"This old frame contains your grandfather's naturalization papers. It's something for our whole family to be proud of. He was so proud to become an American citizen after coming here from the Ukraine."

"Of course, Dad. Don't worry. I'd love to hold on to it." This weathered document proudly announced that my grandfather, Stephen Ladun, was officially a US citizen, and it listed each of his sons on the document and their ages. My father was listed as three years old. Two years later, his father died a victim of typhoid. Granddad was reading the Bible to a gravely ill friend. He must have gotten thirsty with all that reading and sipped water that we would later find out had been poisonous.

Speaking of gravely ill, we found out Dad's heart pains were getting worse. While we were visiting, Dad had a heart exam. Our sister Susan, Linda, me, and Mom went.

It was a precious look that the cardiologist had on his face when he walked into the exam room. He looked like a boy who thought he might be in trouble. "Well who do we have here?" My dad introduced all of us and gave our biography of where we worked and how many children we had.

During the exam, we all had questions. We looked at a discrepancy in one report and a letter from the heart surgeon describing Dad's condition. The conclusion that day was to keep Dad on his nitroglycerin pills and ask him to take it easy. Well, as easy as he could. The man had a Russian Cossack spirit. But he said he'd try to slow down from working in the yard.

Several weeks after we left, Dad got stuck in the yard and was having an attack. He had trouble getting back to the house. He was chopping down a tree. Yep, he was ornery and that was his idea of slowing down! The land he loved so much was an acre and a half. The house was set slightly uphill. With that valve closing down, there was no moving. The nitro did its job again, and he came home to rest, but the attacks were coming faster and with more fury.

One day, Mom was clearly shaken on the phone.

"Your dad fell down today during one of his attacks."

The next day, we got the news that my dad would require surgery. Then another call came to tell us when.

"Brenda?" my sister Linda said in a weak voice.

"Yes."

"Brenda, it's worse than we thought. The surgeon doesn't think Dad should have the surgery. He says the risks outweigh the benefit. Even with surgery, he says Dad could spend his last days in a nursing home."

There wasn't much left to say. "How's Dad taking the news?" I asked.

"He's pretty shaken up," Linda said.

That was enough! I thought. *I'm living in one of the cities with some of the best doctors in the world. I'm going to see if everything humanly possible is being done for Dad.* After some research and contacting a world-renowned surgeon, I was told Dad had only a matter of weeks to live, possibly a few months. That was a blow I can't describe. *It can't be.* This local surgeon reviewed his records and believed he could extend Dad's life.

"Don't delay. Get him here within a week or two," the doctor said.

Living in God's Light

I never thought my parents would agree to come. But the news from this surgeon was shocking and also assuring that he could change the outcome.

We checked Dad into University of Alabama at

Birmingham Hospital. He was well taken care of by a nurse who prepared him for surgery the next morning. I could tell he was a little nervous, but who wouldn't be? Another human being was going to open up his chest.

The surgery seemed to last forever. But finally it was time to talk to the doctor and everything seemed to be fine. Dad had lost some blood during the surgery but that was being controlled. He'd gotten a unit of blood.

Within days he was moved to Lakeshore Rehabilitation Facility just miles down the road from UAB. There he was on the road to recovery. He would get help in learning how to rebuild his strength while also learning how best to take care of himself after surgery. The first order of business was to get him walking. I felt like a proud parent helping him stroll around the hallways.

We had some incredible time together. I really enjoyed listening to his stories. But while we were in that room, we had time to talk about his salvation and forgiving others. Dad was so intelligent; he had so many questions about everything from the beginning of time. He could be a bit of a doubting Thomas at times. But he did believe and love the Lord. I had time to reassure him of his faith. It was a beautiful time.

But one night about 2:00 A.M., I was startled out of my sleep. On the other end of the telephone line was the nurse who had been watching over Dad. She sounded so somber. She said Dad had heart distress;

she'd given him nitroglycerine and had called the ambulance. The paramedics would take him to UAB Emergency.

I sprang out of bed and instantly tried to shake sleep from my head and reached for anything to wear; it didn't matter. I dashed for my keys and purse. About that time Doug was on my heels.

"Wait a minute. I'll drive you," he said.

My mother was sleeping in our guest room. I didn't want to wake her. She, too, had a heart condition. I wanted to get to the hospital and make sure everything was OK, then we'd tell Mom all about what I'd hoped would be a false alarm.

We arrived and waited for the ambulance to get to the ER. Dad came in talking and alert; he even had that boyish grin on his face and chuckled, "Hey, what are you doing here" *Whew! He was going to be alright*, I thought.

The doctor had to run some tests and it seemed we waited in the ER exam room for a very long time. When it was clear the doctor was going to admit Dad for further observation, Doug decided to go back and pick up Dad's belongings, including his glasses.

So there I sat on a little black round stool in the corner of the exam room with my dad just a few feet away. He was hooked up to machines that were beeping to let us all know he was alive. I put my chin in my hands and my elbows on my knees and started to pray. Up until this night, I'd prayed diligently for his healing and for the angels to surround and protect him. I'd prayed for his lungs to clear after surgery. I'd prayed for everything. But at that moment, I couldn't collect my thoughts to form them into words. All I could pray was, "Lord. Oh Lord, Lord, oh Lord."

I kept praying that, and when I opened my eyes, which were directed downward on the floor, I could see the reflection of a bright light. I thought, *That's funny. I don't remember that light being on in here before.* So I sat straight up. I stared straight ahead at the corner of the room. As I did, I saw the bright light in the top of my peripheral vision. I thought, *Wow, that light must be on fire, it's so bright.* Almost afraid to look up, I did. All I saw was a ceiling tile—a dingy one at that. *Whew, I must be tired. That was weird. It seemed so real.* I figured fatigue and stress must have played a trick on my eyes.

Within about 20 minutes, Doug had returned to the exam room with some of my father's personal belongings from the rehab hospital. My father woke up. We rushed to his side. Amid the beeps keeping the tempo of his heartbeat, he started to talk. "I keep seeing these bright lights all around the room."

I started to cry. I thought, *Lord, what is this?* I said, "I know, Dad, I saw one too!" I was trying to comfort him. But I was just as perplexed as he was. I turned and whispered to Doug, "Why am I seeing my father's hallucinations?"

Doug answered, "Why do you do whatever you do?" He was used to me seeing the spiritual perspective. But this was a little above and beyond anything that had ever happened to me. I shrugged it off and was just glad I was able to talk and was certain Dad was going to be OK. I believed it. I prayed for it. Here he was talking and occasionally laughing about something. So when they decided to admit him, I was sure that was just a part of the procedure.

I sat with him all night and into the next afternoon. I went to get my mother to bring her to the hospital. When I called my sister, a nurse, I reported what had happened the night before. I asked Linda if my blood pressure could have caused me to see a bright light like Dad had.

She said she didn't think so. She said, "That sounds strange."

Later, Linda admitted to me she didn't think Dad was going to live much longer. Being a nurse, she often heard about people saying they had seen a bright light before they died. Some scientists claim the light comes from some physiological shutdown of the body. Twenty-two hours later, Dad did pass away just after midnight.

Earlier that night, as I had left Dad, I told him I would bring him the paper in the morning. For the first time in more than a week, he didn't seem excited. I think he knew he wouldn't be there in the morning. He told me to take care of my mother, Doug, the kids, and the dogs.

I had checked with the doctor on the floor and said, "If you think there is any reason I should stay the night I will. He told me, "No. Your father is stable. There is no reason to indicate he'll have any problem tonight. Go home and get some rest."

With a hurricane heading to the coast that night, I knew the next day meant a 12-hour shift, mostly on the news set. My mother and I left the hospital after 10:00 P.M. After midnight, when the phone startled me out of sleep, my first thought was that Dad had had another episode. But the voice on the other end of the line was the doctor who said, "Brenda, I know I said it was OK for you to leave. But your father passed away just after midnight."

"What!" I screamed. No, this can't be true. This can't be happening. This is a nightmare. Please, Lord! Please do something.

"We tried to intubate him. But it didn't work. He was gone. He passed in his sleep gently," the doctor explained.

My heart started to beat as if it were going to jump out of my chest. I thought I was going to have a heart attack. This time I had to wake my mother. I had to tell her. We had to go to see him.

This was the hardest thing I ever had to do in my life. It was all so surreal. Doug grabbed his keys. I called my friend Gwen, who's one of my God-given running buddies. In the middle of the night, she came to watch over the kids while we went to the hospital.

Dad looked very peaceful. We kissed him and prayed over him. We were all in shock.

This was much harder than anything I had been through with cancer.

The hospital chaplain came to pray with us. He kept saying that to be absent from the body is to be present with the Lord. I truly believe Dad is in a better place and that the Lord brought him here to Birmingham partly so Mom wouldn't be alone when he died. It's still hard. But God offered me comfort in sharing with others my story of the light. And I've learned through these years, sometimes healing happens in heaven, not on earth.

Basking in God's Comfort

How do I explain me seeing the light in my father's hospital room? I've consulted local and national theologians. One said to be careful about trying to interpret it. Another said he thought it was God's gift of comfort. In my heart, I believe the Lord knew how hard I worked to keep my father here on this earth. And I did everything in my power to reassure him of his salvation. God knows if I had to pump his failing heart with my own bare hands I would have. I truly believe the Lord gave me a glimpse of the light to comfort me.

In the year since my father's death I believe Satan has tried to get me to blame myself. But each time I get drawn down by doubt, I stop myself and say, *I saw the light!* It was a vision of hope. I know my father is in heaven. I believe it was reassurance. The Lord is good and kind. Some people might think that light experience was a moment of insanity. I believe it's helped me *keep* my sanity because it reminds me God is really in control and He only wants the best for us. Yes, our loved ones have a day and time He has planned for them to pass. We miss them. But with the promise of hope for a future we can all make it here on this earth.

I remember walking back into work. I still had the weight of grief on my shoulders and functioning normally at home or work was difficult. One of the head engineers that I have worked with for 18 years asked if I was OK.

I replied, "God is good." I had to honor my Father in heaven for holding me up when I didn't have the strength to stand on my own. Speaking those words— *God is good*—gave me a sense of peace. God gave me precious time with my father before his death. He also gave me a glimpse of His presence.

While flying back to Birmingham from my parents' home that we were preparing to sell, I clutched my Bible verses. The Lord's Word was the only thing that held me up through my grief.

There was an older woman boarding the same plane. She was struggling with a large, heavy carry-on, so I offered to help. She was so grateful. Then her seat was right next to mine. She thanked me for the help and told me how scared she was to fly. She said her husband used to comfort her, but he had died.

I started to tell her it would be alright and did my best to fill the shoes of a man I never knew. She went on to share the details of her husband's death. Just like my family, she had three daughters. After her husband's heart attack, each daughter used her gift of finance, or of organization, to help this widow to get her affairs in order.

I said, "That's how the Lord works. He provides what we need when we need it."

She agreed. I then felt compelled to tell her about my father and the story of the light and the fact that I truly believe our loved ones are in a better place.

She looked at me as if I had told her I just bought bread and eggs. She said, "I believe you because I also have had a similar experience," and began to explain. She concluded that God had given her a sense of peace that her husband was just fine and had gone on to be with our Lord.

Since then, I've shared the story of the light with several people who had either lost a loved one or were about to lose a loved one. Many have stories of their own. While we grieve because we miss those who have passed from our world, we have assurance in the Bible that tells us we will see them again in heaven.

"The sun will no more be your light by day, nor will the brightness of the moon shine on you, for the

LORD will be your everlasting light, and your God
will be your glory. Your sun will never set again,
and your moon will wane no more; the LORD will
be your everlasting light, and your days of sorrow
will end."

—Isaiah 60:19–20 (NIV)

I decided to share the story of the light because
I hope it will help others who have lost a loved one.
God spoke to me during a warm drizzly day in Janu-
ary. Doug and I were teaching a Sunday School lesson
in our third-grade class. We were reading Matthew
five. It's where Jesus did his Sermon on the Mount and
talked about not covering up your light. I had just been
praying about whether I should share the story. Some
people have told me, "Brenda, that was for you personally." But if the Lord did such a wonderful thing, why
should I hide it.

"You are the light of the world—like a city on a
hilltop that cannot be hidden. No one lights a lamp
and then puts it under a basket. Instead, a lamp is
placed on a stand, where it gives light to everyone
in the house. In the same way, let your good deeds
shine out for all to see, so that everyone will praise
your heavenly Father."

—Matthew 5:14–16

Worship Study Questions

• What hardships in my life can I use to honor the Lord?

_____

_____

_____

_____

• How can I react to pain in my life to honor the Lord?

_____

_____

_____

_____

• What inspirations and blessings can I share to help others?

_____

_____

_____

_____

• How do I feel blessed by sharing with others?

_____

_____

_____

_____

Chapter Nine

Hope and Butterflies

I pray that God, the source of hope, will fill you completely with joy and peace because you trust in him. Then you will overflow with confident hope through the power of the Holy Spirit.

—Romans 15:13

THE HOPE THAT IS NEEDED to survive breast cancer and other troubles we humans encounter can come only from the Lord. You'll remember that Doug and I had to have both of our cars repaired after a recent Alabama storm. The estimate on Doug's SUV alone was more than $6,000. That would be a lot of money out of the grocery budget. And with car repair, one fix often leads to another. It wasn't only that the top and side were dented, there were mechanisms built into the ceiling of the car that had to be disconnected and reconnected. One thing leads to another. Reconstruction after a double mastectomy reminds me of a car repair. One thing did lead to another. I remember wanting someone simply to handle it. Wake me up and let me know when it was over.

But no, I had choices to make, such as which type of implant, what size of implant, and whether I wanted a tram flap, which included a tummy tuck. Then there was the issue of rebuilding the nipples. What color did I want?! Look, I have trouble picking out the color of draperies in my home! But thanks to God, He led me through the whole ordeal.

God Walked with Me

God put Dr. Michael Beckenstein, a great plastic surgeon, in my path. I was rebuilt, like a car damaged after a storm. I may have been "shiny and new" on the outside, with a few scars still left under the paint, so to speak, but I still felt like a wreck on the inside. The fatigue after surgery and chemotherapy left me feeling physically as though I were not hitting on all cylinders. Simply being tired would drag me down emotionally too. I could see why doctors warned about depression as a side effect of cancer. But every step of the way my Lord and Savior was there with me.

He encouraged me through Scripture. He offered hope for a future and, more than that, promised that I had a future. Whether here on earth or in heaven, I knew He had plans for me. He kept telling me that in

His Word. He also encouraged me and offered me hope through people. The Lord used people to deliver food to our home during my illness. He also used them to deliver messages of hope. Whatever seemed to be on my mind that day, He provided an answer for it in Scripture. Quite often it came in the form of a get-well card from believers who included a Bible verse that had lifted them during a time of trial.

> *I will comfort you . . . as a mother comforts her child.*
>
> —Isaiah 66:13

But now, years later, my hope continues to come from the Lord. He showed me my trust and hope in Him is well placed; He will take care of every detail. I know if He carried me through one of the most harrowing storms of my life, He can carry me through anything. He used the whole cancer experience to help strengthen our relationship. That personal relationship and the time I spend with God sustains me through everything in life. And the beautiful thing about growing in Christ is that there is always something new to learn.

Years after cancer, I realize I've come a long way as a Christian, but I also have a long way to go. But even though I know I'm a sinner, I know the Lord forgives me and gives me hope for tomorrow.

Even though I trusted God every step of the way, I still had moments of doubt. I remember the shock, fear, and denial. There was disbelief that this could really happen to the so-called healthy one in the family. I didn't have a heart condition, diabetes, or arthritis. That's why I couldn't believe I had cancer.

This whole ordeal makes me think about how fortunate I was that God doesn't work like an insurance company. There is no cost for a deductible. He doesn't cancel our policy if we call on Him to help us too much. The more we pray and depend on Him, the better He likes it. And there are no stipulations; for example, if the damage to our lives is due to flooding, He still covers it. In fact, whatever the damage comes from, He covers it. No questions asked. By the grace of the Lord Jesus Christ, if we ask, He will listen and help. Even though I had to go through the storm and sustain some "dents" along the way, He polished me, molded me, and restored me to better-than-new condition. He helped me then and He helps me now.

He will help anyone who loves Him, believes in Him, and trusts Him. There is not a complicated contract. Having a personal relationship with the Lord is much easier than signing up for car insurance. My question is this: Why don't more people believe in the Lord? He provides such assurance and security.

Wings of Comfort

One evening at the TV station, while I was tapping away at my keyboard to develop a story, I sensed someone behind me. It was a dear friend whom I had worked with for many years. He had several physical ailments that left him dealing with chronic pain. Almost every part of his body aches at one time or another. For our purposes, we'll call him Joe.

He said he had a butterfly question and wanted to get my take on it. I immediately rolled my eyes and turned around quickly.

"OK, who's been telling you about my butterflies!" I was nearly shouting and laughing, as though I were being ribbed.

"What butterflies?" he said, puzzled.

"I didn't tell you about my butterflies?"

"No," he answered.

"Did the kids tell you about my butterflies?" I asked him.

"No," he responded.

Joe would often be kind to the boys when they would make an appearance at the station. He befriended them and they adored him. We even stopped by to help him with a chore or two because of his health limitations. Joe is a good, kind guy; a believer who loves people. He was an inspiration to me when I was coming out of surgery. I kept thinking, *If he can do it, I can too. If he can drag himself into work for years with several afflictions, I can certainly take chemo and keep on moving.* Joe is truly a brother in Christ; we often have enjoyed discussions about the Word.

"OK, I'm going to ask you again. No one told you about my weird butterfly stories?" I inquired.

"No!" he said. "What about your butterflies?"

I went on to tell him that after my dad died, I kept noticing butterflies. I had remembered how God sent a bird to comfort Elijah. I got a sense of peace whenever I'd see those big, beautiful, yellow butterflies. I had never actually noticed them before. But I figured the grief after my father's death slowed me down a bit and I was looking around more than I had in the past. I had been a work machine and mother of three who always had to be somewhere or do something. But I was stunned and sad over my dad's death.

I kept seeing these yellow butterflies throughout the summer and even when I went to Pennsylvania to help clear out my parents' home and help get my mom moved to Florida with my oldest sister, I kept seeing yellow butterflies. One especially hovered over the dumpster where a lifetime of memorabilia sat cast away. Then my two sisters went to the next town to get some boxes for the move. When they returned, they commented on how many beautiful yellow butterflies they had seen. I got a chuckle and again a sense of comfort out of it.

Another strange butterfly moment came when I returned from a jog in my parents' neighborhood, the place where I grew up. A realtor was at the side door about to knock. I greeted him. The tall lanky man with dirty blond hair shook my hand. While we were exchanging pleasantries, a big yellow butterfly did a figure eight around us and circled the man's head three times. We laughed and both thought it was strange.

Then when I returned home to Birmingham, my middle son, eight at the time said, "Mom something weird happened in the car today."

I said, "What is it?"

He went on to tell me that his dad had the windows down in the SUV and a big butterfly came in and circled around their heads while the car was going at least 40 miles per hour down the road . . . then it flew out.

I was driving from Birmingham to Tuscaloosa to make an appearance to benefit breast cancer, and I took my boys along to see the action. My middle son, Gabriel, said, "Mom, there's a blue and black butterfly following our car."

I said, "What?"

He said, "Yes, and it has been following us for a while now."

I asked him to keep me posted. We pulled into a parking spot and there was the beautiful blue and black butterfly hovering over our car. I wondered if the butterfly was getting a lot of food from the dust on my car. *I really need to wash it more often* I thought.

The next day I told my mother about the charming

little encounter and we agreed it was strange that the butterfly would stick with us through the miles, especially on a winter day.

Mom said, "You know, I just put your dad's picture in that butterfly frame you gave me. You remember what color the butterfly is on it, don't you? Blue and black."

Praise God for the comfort and hope He sends us, even when we don't quite understand it.

God's Transforming Power in Us

Then I was asked to talk about my book and breast cancer awareness on a pastor's radio program. I had asked this same pastor about the light the morning before my father's death. I told him I felt the butterflies to be a blessing and assurance from God. As I was leaving the church, I looked down and saw this huge, fat, black and yellow caterpillar. I knew the next spring he would turn into a big yellow butterfly. And at that moment, the Holy Spirit filled me with a sense of elation.

That's how we are here on this earth. We crawl around in the dirt and sin of the world. When we die and are believers, we become a new and more beautiful being! Thank You, Lord, I prayed. That's how believers are transformed. I would never look at butterflies the same way again. They remind me of the promise of hope we have in the Lord Jesus Christ. He can transform us into a new being from the time we ask Him into our hearts. The transformation continues when we pass from this world to the next to be with Him.

One day, a butterfly of hope came in the form of an email at work. It read that a little seven-year-old girl was planning to give away the money she had saved for a special crystal butterfly. She had been touched by the story of a little two-year-old boy, Jay, with mitochondria disease. It's a condition where the afflicted person is plagued with weak muscles and seizures. When this little girl found out about his plight, she said butterflies aren't that important.

Her mother thought it was a great news story because it was such a selfless act. OK, the truth is that she mentioned a butterfly and I was hooked! I set up the story, agreeing on a time for this little girl to meet Joey. What that selfless little girl didn't realize was that she was not only going to be a part of a warm and fuzzy news story, she also was going to receive the crystal butterfly she wanted, donated to her by Swarovski.

My photographer and I went to the Paulins' home. We were greeted by Joey's mom, Roseanna, a beautiful young mother. Little Joey was watching *Nemo* on television. His mom said, "He loves *Nemo*. That's all he wants to watch." She then picked him up and placed him on the floor. He's an adorable little boy with dark hair and eyes like his mother—strikingly handsome. Joey was so excited to have visitors. He started showing us his stuff.

He could roll across the floor and hook his foot around the leg of a coffee table. His mom told me that doctors said he'd never walk, talk, crawl, or roll. But this determined mom helped this sweet child learn to roll by putting his favorite toys out of reach.

Hope coupled with love helped this little boy do something doctors said he couldn't. As a cancer patient, I was given a laundry list of activities I couldn't or shouldn't do. I am reminded of His Word.

> *You, O God, are both tender and kind, not easily angered, immense in love, and you never, never quit."*
>
> —Psalm 86:15 (*The Message*)

Sometimes it's that last breath or that last bit of effort that wins the prize. If we give up, we don't know how close we were to victory. This young mother, brave and strong, daily faced the possibility that Joey could stop breathing for good. Jay could die from his seizures, accidents caused by weak muscles, or his brain could actually forget to tell him to breathe. She'd called the fire department more than 18 times in two years because Joey stopped breathing. Yet, when I sat there interviewing her, she was calm. "Love never gives up, never loses faith, is always hopeful, and endures through every circumstance" (1 Corinthians 13:7).

After the interview, I presented the little girl with a big crystal butterfly surprise and Roseanna, Joey's mother, with a pin of courage. Then I got a chance to play with Joey. I noticed that he moved pretty well on the floor. He had some muscle tone. He also had a sparkle in his eyes and a beautiful smile. I sat there praying silently for this child. I believe the Holy Spirit led me to ask a question: "Has Joey ever been in water therapy?"

"Well, no." his mother said.

I went on, "It seems to me Joey's muscles aren't the problem; it's gravity that's keeping him down." I remembered seeing astronauts move in space and learning that very small movements would propel them from one place to the next. "If we could just find a way to get Joey into a pool, I wonder what he could do." Roseanna looked at me politely and said she'd try anything. Later she admitted that she thought I was a little strange for making the suggestion. I felt like I was going out on a limb as well. But when the Holy Spirit puts something on my heart, I have to share it.

I made contact with an old friend from the station, Damien Veazey. He once was a producer at the station, now in management at the Lakeshore Foundation. When I explained Joey's condition, Damien said others who'd been told they'd never walk did walk thanks to therapy at Lakeshore. Ah, there *was* hope!

When I told Roseanna they could go to Lakeshore

to check it out for free, she was ecstatic. "I'm willing to try anything," she said.

A few weeks later, my phone rang. It was Roseanna.

"Brenda! It's Roseanna. I just wanted to thank you so much for sending us to Lakeshore! My mother and I watched him as he squealed and laughed in the water. We've never seen him do the things he did today! He loved it! Thank you so much! Keri who worked with him in the water is wonderful! Thank you! My mother and I were both in tears, it was so good to see him be able to move in the water like he can't on dry land." She said goodbye.

I sat there, stunned. Tears filled my eyes. I praised God for the suggestion. I felt like a piece of fiber in God's tapestry. I could see how He used my knowledge and connections to provide this mother with help and hope. I knew she'd been tired. Picking up Joey was hard. But the water made him lighter and allowed his weak muscles to work better.

I understood what it felt like to be weak because of my postoperative experience. I never realized how weak an operation like a mastectomy with reconstruction could leave me. But the second day after I got home from the hospital, I remember asking for a glass of water. One of my dear family members handed me a glass full of water. The cup was a heavy glass and the weight of the water in it was too much for me to hold. When I tried to pull it to my mouth it might as well have been

200 pounds. I could tell Joey had a desire to get up and play. But his body was getting in the way, and gravity was pressing him down.

Joey's mother invited us along to document the progress Joey was making at his second session in the water. He laughed, splashed, and reached for a toy on command. His mother laughed and cried tears of joy. Doctors had told her Joey didn't have many cognitive skills. This proved them wrong. She took video on her camera and said, "I can't wait to show Joey's doctor this! Every time he sees him, Joey's asleep or sleepy." Joey has to take a number of medications to help control the seizures. So by the time she drives him to the specialist in Atlanta, he's wiped out and doesn't respond very well. But this could shed a whole new light on his condition.

Through a series of water-therapy sessions, Joey actually stood up for the first time in his life. It was in the water with a special device. But he stood! The Lord worked in many ways concerning Joey.

I reflect on God's promises when I think about that: "I can do all things through Christ who strengthens me" (Philippians 4:13 NKJV), and "He gives strength to the weary and increases the power of the weak" (Isaiah 40:29 NIV). I believe the Lord has a special mission for Joey— to teach others how to live, love, care, and help each other. Joey's Web site is visited by hundreds of people. Many kind, caring people have touched the Paulins' lives.

People all over pray for Joey. It's in Joey's weakness that the Lord's strength is evident. If the Lord can touch people's hearts and lives through this little boy, how can He use our lives to bring hope to others and glorify Himself?

Daily, my family continues to pray for Joey. When I look at him, I see God's possibilities and pray the Lord to heal him and be glorified through that healing. "With man it is impossible, but not with God; all things are possible with God" (Mark 10:27 NIV).

The Apostle Paul talked about strength in weakness when he prayed three times for the Lord to take away a thorn in his flesh and the Lord answered him:

> *Each time he said, "My grace is all you need. My power works best in weakness." So now I am glad to boast about my weaknesses, so that the power of Christ can work through me. That's why I take pleasure in my weaknesses, and in the insults, hardships, persecutions, and troubles that I suffer for Christ. For when I am weak, then I am strong.*
> —2 Corinthians 12:9–10

The Lord used cancer to strengthen me in a lot of ways, mentally, physically, and spiritually. What I'm most grateful for is the spiritual strength and the depth of hope I have gained, because I know that will last much longer than a lifetime.

Worship Study Questions

• What struggle in my life do I need help with, to have more hope?

_____

_____

_____

_____

• How can I turn from defeat in this situation and look for the hope God offers?

_____

_____

_____

_____

• How should I pray for the hope that I need to help me through this troubling time?

_____

_____

_____

_____

Chapter Ten

Fitness and Fellowship

Don't you realize that your body is the temple of the Holy Spirit, who lives in you and was given to you by God?

—1 Corinthians 6:19

NEWSROOM SOUNDS ARE MUSIC TO MY EARS: People tapping computer keyboards; photographers and reporters rushing in and out as editors busily choose the best video for that night's show; police radios squawking with car accidents, shootings, and domestic dispute reports. Information flows through a newsroom like a river. I've always loved my fast-paced career in this business. No two days are alike.

This day, I looked up from the script I was working on to see Denise, a pretty blonde-haired, blue-eyed, cheerful audio operator who was leading a local church group on a newsroom tour. The group said hello. I waved.

"How are you? Glad you're here," I offered.

They all nodded and smiled. One of the ladies lagged behind the tour group and pulled me aside. She shared with me that she, too, had had breast cancer. I asked her how she was doing and she said after four years she was doing very well except she really missed not being able to sit up on her own in bed.

I asked, "Why can't you sit up on your own?"

She replied, "Because I had the surgery for breast cancer and reconstruction. I had a tram flap."

I said, "I did, too, and I can sit up in bed."

I proceeded to tell her how to adapt some exercises so that she, too, could sit up. I suggested she get with a physical therapist.

For that sweet woman and thousands like her, I wrote this book and taped the companion DVD—to show what goes on behind the scenes of a breast cancer diagnosis, surgery, and recovery. It's to help get the word out that there are amazing advances in the search for cancer cures, and to report what medical experts support: the importance of your spiritual health. Having Jesus with you every step of the way will help you get your life back.

You can do what you did before and feel even better than ever through spiritual and physical disciplines. I also want to emphasize the benefits of fellowship with others who will support you. I'm blessed to be able to run daily with a godly group of women. Before dawn, bleary-eyed, we start out. In my five years since cancer, these women have been encouragers and prayer warriors. But I know not everyone has consistent, committed workout buddies. Still, I want to encourage women who survive breast cancer to exercise. On the news, I often report that studies find exercise not only helps prevent cancer, but also, in women who have been diagnosed and even women with advanced stage breast cancer, those who exercise feel better and live longer.

Doug and the boys agreed to help with the DVD. It became a family project. Interspersed in this chapter are excerpts from the taping that produced the DVD in the back of this book. OK, quiet on the set.

From *Behind the Scenes of Breast Cancer* DVD
with host Brenda Ladun
INTRODUCTION

SETTING: Sunny outdoors, in flower garden
ACTION: Brenda is planting flowers. Her three boys rush through background, and then pitch football to Brenda.

BRENDA: *Welcome to getting your life back . . . and becoming even better than before.*

Since your diagnosis, surgery, and treatments, many people have been telling you what you can't do. I'm here to tell you what you can do and how you can be better after cancer than ever before. I want to share with you God's message to me: "Don't underestimate yourself!"

Just like these flowers I'm planting, you, too, can grow in ways you've never imagined with God's help. In fact, I'm breaking one of the rules; I was told that because of the fact they removed some lymph nodes, I should never garden again. Of course, I was also told I'd never play tennis or hit a golf ball again, I couldn't do sit ups, and I probably couldn't sit up in bed on my own.

And, oh yeah, . . . I should take it easy! That catch represents more than a mom catching a ball. Try raising three boys; there's no taking it easy! Life goes on. All the things I was told I couldn't do, I'm going to show you how you can do them, with the approval of your doctor. Now, let's get started. I remember being fearful that I would hurt the affected arm where the doctor removed lymph nodes. In the beginning, I shied away from playing catch because I was afraid of injury. But with the right strength training and physical therapy, I'm playing catch again.

Remember, before you start any exercise program, you should check with your doctor to make sure it's right for you.

Physical Healing

Playing catch again and getting back to my life required me to get moving. The DVD shows how specific physical therapy addressed my ability to move and to increasingly exercise. This benefited both my body and spirit. Consistency is key to making improvement. A lot of effort early on can prevent a lifetime of problems.

🔘 GET MOVING

SETTING: Hallway outside physical therapist's office.

ACTION: A physical therapist and Brenda do stretches and movements that prevent what is known as frozen arm. The therapist also explains what happens when surgeons remove lymph nodes and the lymphatic system flow can be interrupted. They go on to do several helpful exercise therapies that address lymphadema.

Frozen arm and lymphadema

Lymph nodes are little sacks under the skin that help cleanse our bodies of pollutants or disease. That's why doctors look at the lymph nodes after spotting a tumor of a certain size in the breast. Lymphedema is an abnormal buildup of fluids and cell wastes in the tissues that happens when the lymphatic system is unable to work properly. That can lead to complications like a swelling and possibly an infection of the arm.

There's both primary and secondary lymphedema. Primary is when the swelling happens without any reason. It may be in the arms, legs, or any part of the body.

Secondary lymphedema occurs when some kind of damage happens to the lymph system, such as surgery. If you've had a number of lymph nodes removed, it's good to be aware that you need to take caution with that arm. Avoid cuts, insect bites, and stings. Avoid needles and having your blood pressure taken in that arm. If you do get a cut or an abrasion, be sure to clean the area and use antibiotic ointment with an adhesive bandage.

Keep the arm clean. If you garden or do household cleaning chores, use rubber gloves. Better yet, get someone else to do the cleaning!

You can do daily light massages to get the lymphatic system flowing better. Take the fingertips of your affected arm and make a light circle in the armpit of your good underarm. That clears the working lymph nodes. Then with your good arm, take your fingertips, place them on the shoulder, and pull lightly on the skin from the affected arm toward the other shoulder.

My surgeon told me to keep on running. Experts say about 30 minutes of exercise a day helps to clear your lymphatic system. Running and jumping are the best ways to clear it through exercise.

🔘 WALKING, RUNNING

SETTING: Sunlit walking path through the woods. ACTION: Brenda walks leisurely and is later joined by a fitness specialist. Dialogue explains how to get started

with walking and running and the benefits of drinking water.

BRENDA: *Getting your life back can be as simple as putting one foot in front of the other. You don't have to be a breast cancer survivor to have gotten derailed on exercise. Working, having babies, and raising children takes time. But if we don't take care of ourselves, we won't be able to take care of our loved ones.*

Walk. It's the simplest and most natural form of exercise. Even if you can't get outside right now, you can get up off that couch, and make a difference in your life. Start walking at a comfortable pace. If you're not ready to go outside, walk as long as you can in place while you watch the DVD.

Walking and running became a high priority for me during and after my treatment. I feel better when I get out and go. I felt like I could be miserable in bed or I could get up and walk, and exercise really did help. I asked a physical therapist why I had less pain when I was standing up and walking. The answer: because if you are lying still the pain is all your brain is focusing on. If you are moving—doing a lot of things—the brain has more to process, and less emphasis is placed on the pain alone. I also felt it was cleansing physically, mentally, and spiritually. Walking or running was a good time to pray, and more importantly listen to God.

When exercising, it's important to go at your own pace. Don't try to do too much and get winded. You want to enjoy walking so that you'll want to do it again the next day. The best advice is to start slow. Make it a comfortable pace so that you'll want to walk again tomorrow. Make it enjoyable. For fat burning results, a slower pace is actually better.

Chemotherapy treatments, steroids to help provide strength during the cancer battle, and cancer-suppressing drugs like Tamoxifen all can cause weight gain. I was determined to battle the best way I could. I drank a lot of water. I ate small nutritious meals with very little fat. I also burned more calories than usual by walking and running. Instead of gaining weight, I actually lost weight. I lost so much weight, my doctor asked me to put a few pounds back on. So it is possible to control weight with exercise.

Set goals. When walking or jogging, look at something in the distance, focus on it, and walk or jog to it. I learned that the only limits I had were the ones I placed on myself. While I respected my doctor's advice to take it easy, I also knew taking it easy for too long would only lead to a sedentary life. I wanted to get stronger.

GETTING STRONGER

ACTION: Personal trainer joins Brenda outside the One Nineteen Health and Wellness facility, Birmingham.

BRENDA: *Since cancer five years ago, I've run five and a half marathons. That's something I never dreamed of before cancer. Remember those uphill battles like cancer can make us stronger if we allow God to guide us. Battling cancer and running marathons are similar in a lot of ways. During both you need some supernatural strength to pull you through. Here's one of the Bible verses that helped me and I hope it helps you!*

> *He gives strength to the weary and increases the power of the weak. Even youths grow tired and weary, and young men stumble and fall; but those who hope in the* Lord *will renew their strength. They will soar on wings like eagles; they will run and not grow weary, they will walk and not be faint.*
> —Isaiah 40:29–31 (NIV)

One of my greatest fears came when it was time to carry in the groceries. I actually ached after some of those first trips back to the store. Light and steady weight training helped me get my orange juice and milk in the house without worrying about hurting myself.

We talked about how light weight training can help prevent injuries to the affected arm. All I wanted to do was lift my baby again! Weight training helped me do that, and my two-year-old's words were music to my ears when I lifted him. "Mommy! You're strong again!"

Remember, if you don't want to spend extra money right away investing in weights, you can use cans of soup to start, which will give you a little more resistance and help you build up your strength.

Core training includes the muscles around the body's midsection. I had a tram flap procedure. That means tissue was taken from my abdominal area to help rebuild breasts. One of the biggest challenges was to be able to sit up in bed again.

I regained stomach control by using a large ball big enough to sit on as a sit-up mat. If you don't have one of these at home, a nice wide ottoman or the side of a bed might do very nicely. See the exercises on the DVD. Consistent work along with light weights and moderate sit-ups can improve strength in a matter of weeks.

Sitting up straight is something I took for granted before my surgery. But after surgery it was something I worked very hard to regain.

Good posture can help keep you happy and healthy longer. Poor posture after breast cancer surgery is quite common. A patient tends to guard the area naturally curving to protect it. This can bring on muscle tension and pain. Massage therapy can help this..

MASSAGE THERAPY

ACTION: A massage therapist demonstrates how to get muscles loosened up with a massage.

What about diet? Healthy food is a gift from God. Try to eat more fruits and vegetables. Fish is also high in cancer-fighting oil and salmon has nutrients that fight depression.

🔵 NUTRITION

ACTION: A registered dietitian shows that certain foods help boost energy levels, and other foods help to battle cancer.

Bright-colored vegetables contain more cancer-fighting nutrients. Blueberries are high in antioxidants. Chocolate has also been added to the list. Watch out for the fat content and don't overdo candy bars. It's the dark chocolate that has the benefit since it's lower in sugar and milk. Teas provide good antioxidants too; black and green teas are high on the list. Studies have shown water flushes the body of waste and is also believed to help in fending off cancer. See one of my favorite salmon recipes here and check

> **Brenda's Salmon**
>
> *Take a filet of salmon, pepper it with Old Bay seasoning, drench it in ginger sauce, and then sprinkle sesame seeds on top. Bake for 20 minutes at 375°F, or less if you prefer your salmon more rare.*

out the DVD for some great cooking and recipe tips.

In any good diet, moderation is the key. If you need a snack, instead of reaching for a cookie, reach for almonds or just about any kind of nut. Almonds especially have cancer-fighting qualities.

Don't forget about fiber, which can help prevent a number of cancers. Fiber can help control weight and keep the colon unobstructed. Being overweight isn't just linked to heart disease, high blood pressure, and diabetes. Researchers have found being overweight also increases one's chances of getting cancer.

Spiritual Healing

To help you stay on track with your new health plan, find a positive support group at your church or local hospital. Perhaps there is someone in your neighborhood that needs an exercise buddy. If you can't find a support group, you can always create one. Surround yourself with people who can encourage you. There are a lot of people who want to share their war stories, so to speak, and tell you how hard it is. I found surrounding myself with people who would tell me I could do this or that also helped motivate me.

Remember, whatever you attempt, check with your doctor first and build up slowly. The key word is *slowly*, with your doctor's permission.

The number one encourager is the Lord!

🔘 WORDS FROM BRENDA'S DOCTORS

ACTION: Doctors explain the treatment and surgical advances, and the relationship between spiritual and physical wellness.

I ran my first marathon less than a year after my mastectomy. How is that possible? With God's help you can be better than before—mentally, spiritually, and physically.

> *Forget the former things; do not dwell on the past.*
> *See, I am doing a new thing! Now it springs up;*
> *do you not perceive it? I am making a way in the*
> *desert and streams in the wasteland.*
> —Isaiah 43:18–19 (NIV)

There will be ups and downs on the road to recovery. But with the Lord holding you the entire way, you can rest in knowing He has everything in your life under control. "Trust in the LORD with all your heart and lean not on your own understanding; in all your ways acknowledge him, and he will make your paths straight" (Proverbs 3:5–6 NIV). My prayer for you is that the Lord will use you to go on to inspire and help a sister or brother who's walking the same path. Get up and see how the Lord will amaze you!

God bless!

Praying for Godly Friends

Why is it there are some people you feel like you've known all your life when you first meet them? I believe a friend is a gift from God.

Sharing and communicating can help heal both internally and externally, and even save lives. Talking about breast cancer at your office or church might spur someone to get a mammogram. Reminding people that men can get breast cancer, too, could save a life. Urge other people that any change in their bodies should be checked out. Regular checkups are imperative.

I mention in the DVD that it's important to find an exercise encourager. My husband is encouraging and runs with me. What a great friend he has been over the years! We love going to the gym and shooting hoops together. He has run marathons with me as well. There's nothing like the bonding that happens as I race along with my sweet husband.

Friends and exercise help a cancer survivor feel better. "A friend loves at all times" (Proverbs 17:17 NIV). I found my gifts from God in my morning running group. The Lord led me to them right about the time my treatments were ending. My hair was just coming back in. The children were younger then and the best time for us mothers to run was before dawn. After 8:00 A.M., there were always things that would come up to interrupt a jog. Someone would get sick and have to go to the pediatrician or the dog would have to go to the vet.

It has been rise and shine early to run, at 5:30 A.M., even if the sun isn't quite peeking through yet. I see the ladies in the running group, pounding the golf course path with their sneakers. We discuss the issues of the day. Those who couldn't stay awake for the nightly news ask me to catch them up on the latest. We discuss the problems of the world for 45 minutes. Then I come back to reenter the real world, get breakfast ready, wolf down a bowl of cereal, and shower.

The important thing is not that you run, but that you find an activity that you enjoy and that brings encouragement.

I hope you will pray for the right exercise buddies. God brought me women who are godly, who understand the problems mothers face, and who also provide laughter, which has been proven to be good for the health.

Worship Study Questions

• What is my prayer for my health?

_____

_____

_____

_____

• When can I fit exercise into my day?

_____

_____

• When will I get started?

_____

Date _____ Time _____

• What forms of exercise do I enjoy?

_____

_____

_____

• Realistically, which exercise program could I stick to the best?

_____

_____

_____

• Is there someone in my neighborhood to exercise with to help me be accountable and consistent?

_____

_____

_____

• Where can I meet with a positive support group—at my church or hospital?

_____

_____

_____

Chapter Eleven

Joy in God's Strength

The joy of the LORD is your strength!

—Nehemiah 8:10

T HE WEEK HAD BEEN FULL of breaking news about people murdered, bodies found, and politicians in trouble with the law. The days also had been filled with field trips, school projects, papers, and tests. I had to cut up 350 strips of material for a first-grade art project, send ten dimes in a baggy to my son's first-grade class, make a costume for the play, and make a costume for the book report (making sure the book report was done in good fashion). Throw in a couple of public appearances, reports of my own, writing a book, and producing a DVD, I was exhausted! Sleeping in until 7:00 A.M. sounded unbelievably appealing. Much better than the 5:30 A.M. normal rise 'n shine time during the week. (I know this sounds odd. I don't get much sleep. The only explanation of how I can keep going is God's grace. If He wants me to get up at 5:30 A.M. and go all day until 12:30 A.M., that's what I'll do.)

There I was, enjoying the soft pillow and covers with Copper, our beagle mix, snuggling by my feet. Couldn't have been more perfect. That is, until Garrett wandered in, sleepy eyed, and sandwiched himself between the sheets and comforter. Then, like clockwork, son number two jumped into the king-size bed my husband, Doug, had vacated moments before for an early morning golf game. As many Saturday mornings as he could, this was his ritual with some of his regular golf buddies. Our firstborn wandered in to join us for a few extra winks with the family.

The stillness and quiet didn't last long. I think boys' DNA—at least mine—includes some Mexican jumping beans. Being still for long does not come naturally. I relented and turned on the cartoons. *At least I can still keep my eyes shut while they watch one of their favorite cartoons,* I thought. The boys rustled Copper. He then tried to reclaim a portion of the foot of the bed that had been invaded by boys' feet. He spotted himself in the mirror during this process and started to growl in a low warning for that doggy in the mirror to vacate his territory! Ha! It was one of the funniest sights I'd ever seen.

I wondered what was going through this mind if he could talk. *Hey, you dirty dog get out of here.* Or how about, *Hey, you ugly dog,* or on the other hand, *You good-looking dog!* We'll certainly never know. What we do know is that he was doing no one any good by growling at himself. Copper struggles with ego issues since two rescued golden Labradors we invited to live with us tried to kill him. With small children in our home, we had to find homes for those canines. Since then he wants to be the one and only dog in the household. Who can blame him; he has a great gig. He sleeps 20 hours a day, is fed on time, and has a warm, dry house at his disposal.

Sometimes I wonder if I waste time like Copper, growling and grumbling in the mirror. A conversation at a dinner party the same night Copper experienced his reflection ordeal was enlightening. That evening two people were telling of the problems two different animals suffered after challenging their own reflections.

In the first story, a man was a deer hunter. He knew a big old buck was in the woods near his home. The buck had been rubbing trees, marking his territory. He wanted to chase away any competition for the vegetation in the area.

So the man grabbed two antlers and clanged them together. This made the sound of two bucks vying for the same territory. This enraged the buck. He'd just spent the day claiming this area as his own. So, in the dark, that buck set out to defend his territory. In the meantime, the man went to bed planning to shoot the buck in the morning. He was sure that the animal would be nearby to claim the territory. But instead of finding the big beautiful animal alive, he found him dead in the shallow creek near his home. The buck had jumped into the water headfirst. This longtime hunter deduced that the buck was so enraged that he went looking for his competition that night. Spotting his reflection in the shallow pond, he dove headfirst into the water, slamming his antlers on the bottom, and breaking his neck.

Another woman followed up with the story of a dog. The dog had spotted his reflection in the water and wanted what he thought was the other dog's bone. He dropped his bone and barked at the reflection . . . losing the bone in a creek that washed it away.

Like the buck, the dog was challenging his own reflection. Like these animals, are we sometimes so caught up with our own reflections—our own lives— that we end up losing in the end? Do we lose the joy in life by trying to be top dog doing it our way? In the Bible, the Lord tells us, "Unfriendly people care only about themselves; they lash out at common sense" (Proverbs 18:1).

Bad Reflections

Looking in the mirror almost cost me my life! A dear friend was in the hospital. My sweet husband Doug and I planned to visit him at UAB Hospital, the hospital where my father passed away a year and a half earlier.

I didn't really think about reentering the hospital and the fact that it would bring back a painful memory. We entered the parking garage and of course on this particular day we had to wind around and around to find a parking spot. With each turn, I remembered coming to this parking deck three times a day to visit my father. Then we walked into the hospital at the same place I had to call my sister and brother-in-law in Pennsylvania to give them the news that Dad had died. All the memories came flooding back with each step toward the elevator. The only thing I could almost chuckle about was the fact that a Starbucks had been added to the long corridor entering the hospital. *Well,* I thought, *wouldn't that have been nice during the long hours Dad was here to have a little distraction. But no, we missed it by about a year,* I guessed.

Then to the elevator, where we'd had such hope for a full recovery for Dad before the surgery. Doug, by my side, asked, "What's wrong?" I was welling up with tears. Little did the people sharing the elevator know my dad went home to heaven here more than a year ago. I kept trying to think of something else, but I could only focus on all that had happened there. When the elevator stopped, we got off on a floor much like the one where we had waited to hear the post-op news. I told Doug I had to go into the bathroom and dashed in there to collect myself. I cried, splashed water on my face, and popped a large mint in my mouth to shake myself out of this pity party that my dad would have hated. He always told me not to feel sorry for myself. I was grateful no one was in the bathroom. I could hyperventilate all by myself without someone recognizing me and saying something like, "Hey there, aren't you the lady on television? You look so different when you're hyperventilating and crying like a baby." And choking.

The mint lodged in my throat. I thought, *Wow, here I am wallowing in self-pity and I start choking on a mint because of it. Remind me to add this one to my list of things not to do. Don't suck on a mint while violently gasping for air. I thought, Doug will never come in the ladies' room looking for me. No one seems to be around. I'll have to give myself my own version of the Heimlich maneuver.* You know the one. It's like a scene out of a movie. I tried to cough. *Oh Lord, please don't let me die in this restroom. How sad for the kids. After the Lord helped me with a victory over cancer, how embarrassing to die in the ladies' bathroom, choking on a mint. That would be a terrible lead story.* "News anchor dies in bathroom while sucking a mint into her airway."

Finally the mint shot out of my airway and into the sink. I checked the mirror. I wasn't even blue yet. Praise God. *I'd hate to visit our friend and have to explain why I was blue. I, after all, was there to cheer him up!* I headed for the door, to rush to Doug to tell him the good news. I'm alive! I survived a long choking incident. "Hey honey, . . . " I looked around to an empty waiting room. *Oh my, he has the keys,* I thought. *Well, I'll look in our friend's room to see if he is there.* A few turns and a door later, there was

Doug chatting with our dear old friend who'd had a long series of surgeries and conditions that seemed to build one on another. *Wow, I wonder how long I would have laid dead if the mint had gotten me. Probably at least an hour.* Our friend Bubs was a talker and Doug was engaged in serious sports talk.

I realized the Lord had shown me that my own self-pity and looking in the mirror of my own loss almost lead me to a deadly end. I needed to focus on this man lying in the bed who was probably scared and tired of being in a hospital. That was my mission on this day, not a pity party. *I should be ashamed of myself.* I stood in that room and prayed for the Lord's forgiveness for being so self-absorbed.

By focusing on the Lord and not on being the head deer in the forest, or the dog with the biggest bone, or the person with all the sorrow, how much more effective can I be for the kingdom of God? The Bible tells us not to look back at the past but ahead. Now I know why. I can only get stuck in the muck of pain and sorrow if I continue to hold on to the past. Instead of it leading to destruction or heartache, I should be busy about our Father's business and not my own. I can have confidence in the Lord, not in the flesh or earthly things. Then I can find peace by crawling into my Father's lap and letting Him be in charge. Instead of challenging that reflection, whether it be my own shortcomings that are growling at me or the image of a brother or a sister who's disappointed me, peace comes by embracing and loving the image because it's God creation.

> *Forgetting the past and looking forward to what lies ahead, I press on to reach the end of the race and receive the heavenly prize for which God, through Christ Jesus, is calling us.*
>
> —Philippians 3:13–14

Troubles and Joy

After visiting Bubs, I was supposed to meet my dear friend Brenda Clark and a friend of hers at a local pizza restaurant. I was running just a few minutes late after the choking incident and the hospital visit. I joined the ladies' conversation in progress. Brenda introduced her friend, who was being treated for breast cancer and had a number of other things recently go wrong in her life. Brenda thought I could inspire her. *Ha,* I thought, *A woman who gets upset and chokes on a mint is not a pillar of strength.* But if I could help, I would. While I sat and listened to her story, I heard how she not only had breast cancer, but had suffered a heart attack, and actually clinically died momentarily. Her brother died recently after he'd helped take care of her. Her list of troubles went on but she was still working, smiling, and living. She, too, leaned on the Lord for strength. *Lord, forgive me for focusing on my own self-pity. This day was to be about ministering to others and Satan tried to get between that by making me focus on my own reflection.*

But she, with her heavy load, ministered to me that day. She was submitting to God and letting Him guide her, day by day. We both agreed she, too, had a mission to help others who would travel her same path. She was a nurse and said she now could empathize with patients on almost every level; diagnosis, treatment, and even death.

If you love God and put Him first, everything else in life falls into place. "'Love the Lord your God with all your heart and with all your soul and with all your mind.' This is the first and greatest commandment. And the second is like it: 'Love your neighbor as yourself.' All the Law and the Prophets hang on these two commandments" (Matthew 22:37–40 NIV).

If I focused on everything I lost in the last five years I wouldn't be able to get out of bed. I could not own the joy that the Lord clearly promises in His Word. Is it easy to get stuck looking in the mirror of what's wrong with my life? Yes, but with God's help and turning it over to Him and accepting His will in my life, I can find the blessings.

Through the hurts of the last five years, I had to learn to forgive myself. Forgiving and letting painful memories go and letting God control my life is simply healthy. There's no need for stress. In recent years, scientists have discovered what God has been telling us in His Word for centuries. Take care of your body. Your body is a temple. How you take care of it glorifies Him. Stress releases bad chemicals in your body that can hurt your heart, lead to high blood pressure, and possibly even cancer. By resolving conflict with others and in your own life, you can reduce the stress in your life.

That doesn't mean sweep problems under the rug or let them fester. The Lord has told us not to let the sun go down on our anger (Ephesians 4:26). We need to deal with conflicts on a daily basis. Don't deal with them in a hurtful or combative way, but talk it out. That's healthy. Resolving conflict actually has a feeling. You can feel pressure lift off your body, "off your chest," as they say. I'm throwing away regret. I'm releasing myself of the worry about what caused my cancer, and from the worry of the what ifs in life. The Lord is always there with His Word and His power to save us from ourselves.

A cancer diagnosis can lead to self-destructive emotions, such as feelings of envy of others and depression. Studies show depression runs rampant among cancer survivors. Ironically, many of us are given another chance but can let fear of recurrence and not measuring up to life's standards get us down. Even my own family members can't understand the place that I've been . . . from which the Lord alone can deliver. I had a double mastectomy, chemotherapy, lost my hair, then had to take a cancer-fighting drug for five years that was supposed to bring on depression, blood clots, and more side effects than I can count. Do they not understand the pain, fear and responsibility of surviving cancer? No, and who can blame them?

Until you've walked on that cancer path, it's hard to understand. Pain and fear may be easier to understand than the responsibility. I believe I went through cancer to help ease the pain for others. I pray that my experience does in some way offer hope. I know I need to warn people about cancer, but I also need to warn them about the side effects.

The depression and doubt about a future can be wiped away by having faith in the Lord Jesus Christ. I need to get things done my way. But there's that reflection standing in the way I get hung up on. I get hung up on what I think needs to be done. What I think needs to happen. How imperfect I really am. I'm reminded when I get frustrated with God's refining of my life, even through cancer, that everything will pass away but what will last forever is our relationship with my Lord. I have to submit to Him daily and remind myself His plan is better.

I get so busy trying to do what I think I should do on this earth, but we should seek first the kingdom of heaven and not all the worldly things we think we should do or achieve. If we accept that God is in control and let Him be in control, we can start enjoying life. If we accept God's gifts here on earth and digest His Word, we can find peace and joy.

Because of the LORD's great love we are not consumed, for his compassions never fail. They are

new every morning; great is your faithfulness. I say
to myself, "The LORD is my portion; therefore I will
wait for him."

—Lamentations 3:22–24 (NIV)

I was reading a bedtime story to my youngest son. It was a story by Max Lucado called *You Are Mine*. In the story, these little wooden people get so caught up in the things they can hoard for themselves that they lose the joy in life. They put all their effort and hope in their earthly treasures instead of putting all they are in their maker's hands.

It reminded Garrett and me how people get so caught up in things that they want. Our house is filled with toys and video games. Our closets are filled with clothes and shoes. All this stuff gets moved about. Then we have to deal with it. I have to pick it up and put it away. I have to make sure all the clothes we dirty get clean. Sometimes I just feel like opening the door and putting a sign in the front yard that reads, "House sale, I want to declutter my life."

For a while, I was obsessed with the idea of buying a lake house or a farm. I just wanted a refuge for our family to enjoy one another. I've always been concerned about family time, but since cancer I've become even more driven to spend precious time with them. Another motivation for a lake house may be to escape the responsibilities of the home we live in, the laundry and clutter. The Lord opened my eyes through some dear friends with lake houses. They reminded me it's the burden of the first home times two. There are still dishes to clear, walls to paint, dirty clothes to deal with, probably more due to the beach towels. The bottom line is the more you have, the more you have to manage. That was the point of the children's story. The more we collect here on earth, the more burdensome that stuff becomes. Pretty soon all those things we think we want become a heavy load. But the one thing that's never burdensome is a relationship with our maker. "Those who hope in the LORD will renew their strength" (Isaiah 40:31 NIV).

As believers, we know that those who have afflictions on this earth will be healed in heaven with a perfect body. There will be no sorrow. As a newscaster, I see a lot of the horror stories and tears. I know firsthand that after a health calamity or a death of a loved one, there are so many ways I can beat myself up and torture myself. For example, what could I have done differently to have avoided this mess? Lord what should I have done differently? The answer came to me in the form of the Lord's light.

Hours before my father passed, I believe that light was one of the promises of hope that the Lord had everything under control and I should trust Him no matter what. When I trust Him and keep my eyes on Him, I feel empowered and encouraged. But when I take my eyes off of Him and allow doubt and fear to rule me, I feel consumed by darkness.

Living by Grace

He is in control. I must submit to His plan and understand His plan is better. Only then can I truly relax and start really living well, not just living from task to task. What peace I can have—with myself and others—if I simply submit to God's will! Move on past the mirror; don't get mesmerized by an image you want to quarrel with. "What is causing the quarrels and fights among you? Don't they come from the evil desires at war within you?" (James 4:1).

The best thing my dad ever taught me was to stop feeling sorry for myself. Where does it get you? Nowhere fast. Focusing on our own inadequacies can bring even the strongest warrior down fast. Remember David and Goliath. David focused on God and against all odds brought down the giant.

By the Lord's grace I know I've been allowed to stay here and see my boys grow. That's the first thing I thought of when I was diagnosed. How long will I have with my children? So I'm very grateful I was able to see my boys play football and soccer this year. They went from a baby and two boys under ten with a mom who was weak because of cancer treatments, to a first, fourth and seventh grade soccer and football players with a mom who can run marathons. If this sounds like a milestone, it is.

Try this, put your hand in the air and say, "Lord I'm turning it all over to you. I'm turning over every detail of my life to you and I'm allowing you to take the wheel and be in control." I guarantee less control on our part and submitting to the Lord will astound you.

What a great and wonderful God we have! He asks us to give Him our burdens. If we trust and have faith, He will handle everything. Our God doesn't say, "It's your problem; handle it on your own."

One of the scariest moments of my life was when I was in college and asked my mom and dad about a career choice. Their answer was, "We don't know. You will have to decide. I was on my own. But I could still go to my heavenly Father in prayer and ask Him to lead me. He did then and continues to lead me today.

With my boys, I've tried to encourage and inspire them to be the best they can be. But one day while watching my oldest son snap the ball for his seventh grade football team, I realized he was doing it with precise perfection. My husband and others had been saying what a great center he was. I thought, *Oh, they're all being nice.* The coach even told him he was the best. Again, it's great for a mother's ears but I thought, *These people are so encouraging.*

Well, that day my heart swelled with pride in my chest as I watched his flawless performance on the football field. I realized, after all the mothering I'd done over the years, I was not in control of this child. This was the Lord's child, loaned to me for a while. As hard as I prayed during sporting events for him, I realized while I was sitting on the bleachers just watching, I couldn't help him in this, only God could help him.

The Lord had given a talent to this young man that I never knew existed. I submitted and said, "Lord, thank You. This is truly Your child."

I realized at that game, no matter what became of me the Lord was in control of this little life. I was not. Even if my body gave out, the Lord Jesus Christ was in Brooks's corner holding all the power this child would need to get through life. Even though as parents we had the responsibility to guide him, he was truly in God's hands.

But isn't that true of everything in our lives? As much as we'd like to think we are in control or calling the shots or trying to make a child into a prodigy, it's really God's plan that prevails that is best. That was a humbling moment as a parent. This recovering type-A personality was put in her place again that day.

While working on the DVD for this book, my husband and I went to St. Vincent's to interview Dr. James Cantrel, my oncologist, and Dr. Susan Winchester, my surgeon. For years, I've been sharing their wisdom with women who call for encouragement through their own cancer struggles.

Doug set up lights and carefully placed the camera on the tripod and focused on Dr. Cantrel outside of the St. Vincent's Chapel. The reason for this was that our project communicated hope through faith. And on this day, Dr. Cantrel delivered a message of hope that I never thought I'd hear in my lifetime. Dr. Cantrel said that in our children's lifetime, he believes researchers will find the cure for cancer. I almost came out of my seat and hugged him. He's usually conservative when it comes to talking about cures. Even mentioning the word *cure* is unusual, because he knows that so many hang on his every word, looking for hope. He is not one to dish out false hope.

But recently the cancer authorities of the country have offered new hope. The Cancer Institute, which compiles data, has concluded we are very close to a cure. The progress in cancer research is exponential, much like what has happened in the world of technology. The progress is rolling faster and faster, kind of like a snowball. He said with a new vaccine for a *papillomavirus* along with many other tiny victories for other types of cancer, he and others believe these pieces of the puzzle will be filled in soon.

God is good. He is allowing us to put the pieces together. With more known about DNA and how God made us, we are starting to have the key to unlock the mysteries of cancer and ultimately how cancer can be defeated. Is God guiding and leading researchers? Yes. I pray for them and ask that you pray for them as well.

Next we had the chairs set up in the balcony of the chapel. We had the beautiful stained glass windows behind Dr. Winchester. As you view the DVD, that setting is no accident. Because Susan Winchester is one of the most spiritual doctors I've ever encountered. The Lord truly used her spiritual guidance to help lead me through my battle with cancer.

During the interview, she reminded me how I had submitted to the Lord that day of surgery. I had to. I knew He was the only one who knew how my book would end. I knew He was the only one truly in control. That moment of submission and trust began a new spiritual growth that hasn't stopped in the years since that surgery. I remember truly relaxing and feeling good just moments before surgery. I wasn't panicked or horrified. I rested in my Father's arms and He hasn't let me down since that moment of surrender. I realized He'd been in control all my life even though I'd fought Him like a defiant teen at times. Ultimately, His will prevailed.

But during the interview, Dr. Winchester said something so powerful that it helped me understand as a caretaker and a patient. No one can go into surgery with you and help you. No one can go into the fire of recovery with you either—no one except for the Lord. Your God is in you and experiences everything you feel. He is in that surgery with you. He walked this earth as a man and understands sorrow, pain, temptation, and everything we feel. He can live in our hearts and go through it all with us. The people we love and who try to take care of us can't jump inside our bodies and help us through. No one can do such a miraculous feat but the Lord Jesus Christ. That thought empowers me in every walk of life. No matter what battle we have, the Lord is in us helping us through it.

> *Now listen, you who say, "Today or tomorrow we will go to this or that city, spend a year there, carry on business and make money." Why, you do not even know what will happen tomorrow. What is your life? You are a mist that appears for a little while and then vanishes. Instead, you ought to say, "If it is the Lord's will, we will live and do this or that." As it is, you boast and brag. All such boasting is evil. Anyone, then, who knows the good he ought to do and doesn't do it, sins.*
>
> —James 4:13–17 (NIV)

Are we a vapor? That verse came to my mind lately while I was looking at a property. I've always thought it would be fun to fix up a big old house. It was seemingly a great deal. There was a house, a mansion really, for sale for about $300,000. It looked like a house that would go for a couple of million if it was in a different location. It was all brick with huge white pillars in the front. It was grand, except for the fact that it was built in 1969. In its day it must have been a magnificent place. I could just imagine the parties they must have had there.

But as I inspected it, I noticed on this rainy gray day, a portion of the brick in the back of the house looked soaked. I'm no construction expert, but I imagined the rain was soaking the wall behind the brick. I also noticed several doors and windows that were severely rotted. Since I love history, I had to ask the story behind this grand old mansion.

As with almost every experience in my life, the story went back to cancer. The original owner built this home then died a few months later of lung cancer. I could only imagine his excitement in building such a dream home. Then he didn't have much time to enjoy all the time and money he poured into it. As I stood looking at the wood crumbling from the ravages of time and moisture, I thought how temporary this life is. We pour so much time and energy into things that don't last. I look back on the last ten years of my life and see how furniture, clothes, and homes crumble.

The one thing that doesn't crumble but gets stronger with time is God's relationship with us. We have an assurance to live with Him forever. Jesus said to His mother while on the cross that He would make everything new. I'd rather accept that promise than put my hope in things of this world that will eventually pass away.

Accepting what we can't change and looking for God's molding through it is one way to find peace. Accepting God's plan for our lives is hard. Our trials may include sickness, job loss, or death in the family. These are all thing that are hard for us to handle on our own. But the good news is that we don't have to handle anything alone. But as I've said, I've learned over the years, sometimes that healing happens in heaven, not on earth. Submitting to His will and accepting His promises can give us hope and peace. Letting go and saying, "God, You know best," is such a relief.

Worship Study Questions

• What is it in my life that I need to accept that is God's will?

_____

_____

_____

_____

•What can I do to submit to Christ, knowing He is in control?

_____

_____

_____

_____

• How can I pray about this situation to help me accept it and submit to God?

_____

_____

_____

_____

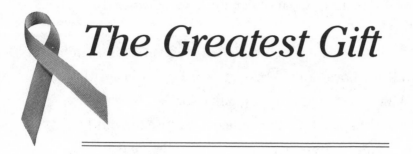

Chapter Twelve

The Greatest Gift

Love is patient, love is kind.

—1 Corinthians 13:4 (NIV)

LOVE IS MENTIONED in the Bible hundreds of times. Love is one of the most important lessons I believe cancer has taught me. I went from simply existing to learning that people love me and God loves me. That healed me inside and out, faster than any medicine could. I also feel that God has increased my heart's desire to love Him more, and to love others more deeply.

I remember reciting "Love is patient, love is kind" (1 Corinthians 13:4 NIV) to myself repeatedly while driving one day during my cancer ordeal. I had been taking Tamoxifen, the drug to suppress hormones and thwart any possible cancer left in my body. For years I had fought the drug's side effects of depression, weakness, and irritability. We all know it's hard to be a working mom, wife, homemaker, and more. That was accentuated by Tamoxifen. I felt as though God sustained me through prayer and His Word, and so I would recite this particular Bible verse when I felt the drug's effects.

While I repeatedly recited this verse as I drove, with my boys in the backseat of the car, I heard Garrett ask Gabby, "What's she doing that for?"

I chuckled. Gabby replied, "Because it helps her."

"Mom! Stop; that's silly." Garrett demanded.

I said, "Garrett, Bible verses help us through tough times."

A few weeks later, we were in the car again making one of our runs. This day, Garrett had misbehaved to the point that he was now in trouble. I believe he even hit his brother while in the backseat of the car. I said in a stern, motherly tone, "That's it Garrett, you will be punished when we get home! I've let this go and you are out of hand."

From the backseat I heard him repeat, "Love is patient, love is kind. Love is patient, love is kind!"

I had to laugh. It had seemed silly to him when he'd heard me recite Scripture. Now, in his crisis, he was asking for mercy with the punishment that was about to befall him. He was reminding *me* to act lovingly.

God's call to love throughout the Bible reminds us to act lovingly.

Love covers a multitude of sins.   —1 Peter 4:8

Love your neighbor.   —Matthew 22:39

Love the L<small>ORD</small> *your God.*   —Matthew 22:37

Christmas is one of the special seasons when we show our love for one another as we reflect on His love. For me, it is in early November when my search to find the perfect gifts for my loved ones intensifies.

One August, however, I dashed into a store during my dinner break. I was on the way home to get a quick bite with Doug and the boys but had an errand to do and it couldn't wait. As I entered the store, I was floored and filled with a sinking feeling.

There in front of me was a Christmas tree. I had to stop to ask myself if I'd missed a few months. Yes, I was sure it was August; I could still wear white shoes! We hadn't even gone back to school, enjoyed Labor Day, or Halloween. Yet, here mocking the fact that I was still trying to get my kids ready to go back to school was a tall, bushy, green Christmas tree! If this had been a movie, I would have expected music from *The Twilight Zone* to start playing. It was bizarre that there was a tree sitting in the middle of the Birmingham metro area in August. I've heard of rushing the season but this was ridiculous.

What made my stomach turn was that someone in their greed had decided to rush the season to make consumers feel the need to hurry to buy Christmas wrapping paper, bows, ribbon, and presents. I hadn't even bought school supplies yet! Don't get me wrong. I've always loved Christmas. Most people do. But since I've had cancer, making it to another Christmas is a cherished milestone. Christmas is the day we celebrate our Lord coming to this earth to save us from our sins. I think that too much emphasis is placed on the perfect tree instead of the true meaning.

On another day, I stopped to realize that each of us may enjoy about 80 to 85 Christmases on this earth—that's if the Lord grants us those years. So I pray for a great warm and loving Christmas every year. Will I look back on my life and say, "Wow, I loved that sweater I got for Christmas?" Doubt it. I look back and remember the smiles on the faces of my husband and children and the laughter and warm feeling of us spending a special day together to celebrate God's love for us and our love for each other.

I cherish every Christmas past cancer because I remember when I was diagnosed, I wondered whether I'd make it to the next Christmas. I wondered who would shop for the boys. Who would wrap the presents? Would Doug search high and low for that hard-to-find toy? Now with each passing Christmas, I'm more convinced that it's the love we show for each other that's most important.

During this past Christmas season, I was caught up in the frenzy to help Santa find that perfect toy. It was a special video game unit that was very hard to find. Many people were camping out overnight to get a chance to buy one. Some people sat outside in the cold all night to be told hours later at dawn that the store had run out of the units.

On the news we reported violence related to people trying to get their hands on this video game. Someone even got shot over one. Another person got trampled. People actually pushed and shoved and walked over another human being to buy a video game! Is this the meaning of Christmas? Greed? That's certainly not how God wants us to spend Christmas or any other day, getting anxious and downright mean over what does not matter.

Nonetheless, I felt the panic of trying to find that video game unit. The hunt for the toy began to rob me of my peace and joy. All I could think of was the toy and how to maneuver to get one. I drew the line at camping out on the street. But I did go to several stores first thing in the morning and then late at night. I even stood in a line of 30 people, only to find out I was number 31 and they only had 30 game units. I was almost relieved because I thought someone might jump me in the parking lot to get my purchase.

Wrapped Up in His Love

Finally, I was sickened that I'd let a corporation's video game consume me with want. I surrendered and said, "God, forgive me. I'm not getting one." At this point, if I'd gotten one for Christmas, I'd have felt dirty. I was so wrapped up and obsessed with having a toy. That was not of God. It's as if Satan tries to rob us of our joy by getting us all riled up about anything that, in the end, won't matter to God.

God tells us that love is the greatest goal. We are to love Him first, and love others, our neighbors, as ourselves. He made us to love. He calls us to love. What is the true measure of this love? It's the person who will stand by you when you are at your worst. God delivered a wonderful man to stand by me in my times of trouble. Even through my heartache and fussiness, fear, and doubt that I could be loved or lovable, the Lord delivered an encourager. I lovingly call him my knight in shining armor, my husband. He provided a shoulder to cry on, and was a rock when I needed him. In good and bad times, as we had promised in our marriage vows, in sickness and in health, he has been there with me.

When I couldn't go to the grocery store, Doug did. He even learned how to cook! The morning after chemo, I lay there wondering how I could get up to make the boys' breakfast. Then I heard a racket coming from the kitchen: pots and pans banging, then sizzling, and then, voilà, the smoke alarm. Yes, Doug put his chef's hat on to take on breakfast duty so I could rest a few more minutes. And one blessing in this is that his eggs are better than any I've ever made.

The Lord also provided some wonderful, real,

godly friends. I mentioned them earlier. These are women who love me enough to tell me when I'm wrong. Through prayer, God put them in my life. They taught me to laugh at myself. They also showed and helped me to understand how to get closer to God. They became even more than friends—they are my sisters in Christ. Gwen Pierce, Brenda Clark, Lisa Weaver, Denise Lowery, Rebecca Touliotis, and Sarah Saul became prayer partners as well as running buddies. When we prayed together, we could see the results. When my father died, they took over planning the after-service meal. My house never looked so good. There were candles burning, and a meal that Rebecca and the girls helped to cater. It looked to me to be similar to something you'd get at the White House for a special dignitaries' event. God puts those you need in your path if you seek Him.

God is love, and without Him love would not exist. Of course, I have to chuckle at that statement; we wouldn't exist without Him either.

> Because he loves me," says the LORD, "I will rescue him; I will protect him, for he acknowledges my name. He will call upon me, and I will answer him; I will be with him in trouble, I will deliver him and honor him. With long life will I satisfy him and show him my salvation.
> —Psalm 91:14–16 (NIV)

Called to Love

My dear friend Gwen Gorby and I have been through a lot together. I'd been working with her for almost 20 years when the unthinkable happened. We'd already been through life's ups and downs together, job changes, and loved ones' deaths (including friends and co-workers). We had talked each other through pregnancies and heartbreaks. I always felt as though Gwen is a precious sister. She, too, loves the Lord. Looking back, we've been in the same little boat for two decades. We've shared a lot. But I noticed she had become withdrawn. I knew there was something up at home, but I could tell she didn't want to talk about it. So I left it alone and gave her the space I thought she wanted and needed. But one day, as I was walking into the double doors at the station, a friend who produced the 5:00 P.M. news said, "Did you hear about Gwen?"

By the grave tone in her voice, I thought she'd been killed. I was afraid to ask, but I did anyway, "What is it?"

She went on to tell me Gwen had been hit by a car while riding her bike on a mountainous road that morning. She had a broken pelvis, back, and leg injuries. But she was alive. Praise the Lord! I also found out there were no head and neck injuries, which was a blessing. In shock and disbelief, I went to my desk to sit down. I couldn't concentrate on email, or script editing at that moment. Before I had time to think about it, I grabbed my purse and was heading for the door. I've got to go see Gwen. I prayed all the way there that she would be alright, healthy and recover. She had a little boy as well. He needed his mom. In fact, she was a single mom.

We really should appreciate every friend every day. Life is so unpredictable and we just never know what will happen tomorrow.

I was afraid of what I would see when I walked through her hospital room door. And, praise God, even though she was clearly hurt, as she lay there in bed, her head and face were as pretty as they always had been. Her hair prettily framed her thin face. She looked up at me with her big brown eyes full of excitement and a beautiful smile. She was actually able to speak! *Praise God!* I thought.

When she opened her mouth to form the words, I thought she would talk about surviving the accident. Oddly enough, her first words to me after being hit by a car were these: "You may think this is bad but this is not bad. I've been through a lot worse with my marriage troubles."

I felt my eyebrows knit and almost was set back on my high heels. I knew Gwen was going through a private turmoil before the accident. I simply didn't know how bad it had been for her. She went on to explain her painful marital breakup. The pain in her body wasn't nearly as bad as what her heart had endured recently. But, she said anytime she tried to move, or someone touched her, she felt like screaming. We prayed that God would show her how much He loved her and heal her inside and out, revealing her blessings through this tragedy.

I listened while Gwen poured out her heartaches of the past year. We agreed that God would show her how much He loved her and would take care of every detail of her life. And He did as He has promised in His Word, "And we know that God causes everything to work together for the good of those who love God and are called according to his purpose for them" (Romans 8:28).

While lying in that hospital bed, she had so many friends from work and neighbors show her the love of Christ through their actions. She had meals planned for weeks, money collected for bills, and offers of help and encouragement from people she barely spoke to over the years. The outpouring of love and the miracles God provided to encourage her was overwhelming. She also got the good news that she would walk again. This time, she'd have God's love holding her up. She had to submit to God and accept His love. And even though her body had been broken, this was the beginning of the healing for a hurting soul. Ironically this accident helped her get past the mirror, so to speak, of heartache. The Lord is certainly gracious.

Do you wonder whether Gwen possibly had been on morphine when she was having this revelation? No. The revelation and the encouragement from God came before the painkiller was ever administered. She later told me she felt God's presence calm her in the ambulance. She strongly felt Him.

Gwen explains what had happened to her this way: She had decided to go ahead and take her daily bike ride as she had for many months because the fog had lifted on that October morning. She was enjoying the cool morning air. Then she heard and saw a van and the next thing she knew, she heard a very loud noise. She was part of the loud noise. The van didn't break until after it had hit her. She rolled up onto the hood, broke the windshield, and her body broke the side mirror off the car. The mirror hit the ground and sliced a tired. That's when the vehicle came to a halt.

She was completely conscious the entire time. She even remembers the rescue crew decided they couldn't airlift her because of the high-level fog. Even though it had lifted from the ground, it was still hanging high enough to prevent the chopper from coming to her rescue.

Gwen said, "I remember the people standing around me while I lay in my neighbor's yard. They wanted to try to move me because ants started crawling all over me. I told them not to worry because I couldn't feel them. When I got to the hospital there was no evidence of ant bites. But I remember thinking when I hit the ground that I was going to die. I couldn't breathe at first. But I realized later I had the wind knocked out of me.

"I was aware of everything. I remember giving the paramedics my former husband's name and phone number to call in order to take care of my son. It might have been easier for me if I had been knocked unconscious. I remember how the rescue crew had trouble getting me onto the board to transport me. I endured excruciating pain any time they touched me. When they finally got me into the ambulance, I could feel every bump on the way to the hospital. I was shaking uncontrollably. I could hear the hum of the ambulance and the road noise very loudly.

"I even heard the traffic noise very loudly. It seemed to ring in my ears. But then it faded away, and everything went surreal. A calmness came over me. Then I spoke to God. I said, 'I can't do this; I'm a single mom. I can't be sick. I can't be injured. I live in the country, and I have animals to take care of. Who will feed them?'

"After talking it over with God, I felt the pain diminish. I didn't hear a booming voice, but I felt the message. God made it clear to me—*'No, you can't do this, but I can.'* I understood and felt Him. I felt Him letting me know that I would be healed and He commanded me to allow Him to be in control. His strong presence reassured me. I definitely felt His powerful presence."

God's Love Heals Us

This accident was the first step in releasing Gwen from a prison of sorrow created by her turbulent marriage. When I walked in her room, it was all about the heartache of a marriage gone wrong, not about coming close to death by being hit by a car!

Gwen had tried at first to negate that God was in control. When asked who could be called, she responded, "No one." She believed she had no living soul who could come to her rescue and help. Sure, she had no family in town, and her former husband who was not concerned with her care. But God would overwhelm her with His love and commitment to her. He would raise up the people who truly loved her. She was not alone. People showered her with love and gifts. The greatest gift He gave her was opening her eyes to His love. Now she could see.

Gwen says, from the time she got in the room, people who cared about her started to pour in. I remember feeling a supernatural pull to go to the hospital. Usually I wait a day to two or until the person goes home from the hospital, because I remember being so tired in the hospital and people would come to visit again and again and it was hard to garner strength to visit with them.

Gwen thought to herself, *I've spent ten months mourning because a man didn't love me, but now I'm being shown that so many people love me and above all God loves me!*

Gwen says she had allowed her circumstances to drag her down. She hopes by sharing her story it will help others avoid the same pitfall of life. Feeling down on ourselves is not of God. Gwen had a reawakening about the people in her life. They cared! My on-air colleague at ABC 33/40, James Spann, came to the hospital. He had much wisdom for Gwen. But something he said especially had meaning.

James said he felt led to say to Gwen: "You have been given a phenomenal gift from God. For years God has had different plans for you and your gift of art."

Gwen is a talented artist and her paintings touch the soul. She knew then that God had plans for her.

During Gwen's reawakening, she says she accepted the fact that her body did not belong to her. She said, "I realized it was God's and I can't keep me. He puts me where He wants me to be and I'm to be content wherever I am. He won't move me until I learn what he wants me to learn."

She went on to explain with her excited eyes about working at the TV station, "I know the Lord wanted me to set foot in the TV station, so He would get the glory. He wanted all those people who were praying for me to know that He did this. He healed me."

God showed His love through one of the worst experiences of her life. Somehow it's hard to fathom, but it took a life-threatening accident to draw her closer to Him and open her eyes to how good and loving He is and how many people truly care about her. I believe the doctors had their part in Gwen's healing certainly, but more than that God provided her with His love through so many of His people. It's the love more than anything that gave her the will to live. Her record recovery, the fact she can walk, and that she exceeded all expectations during physical therapy is more proof that God heals through love. But more than that, the good Lord healed her inside and out. She agrees, it was a healing of the body, mind, and spirit—total healing.

It's as if He had to "blow up the house to rebuild it."

Her healing alone is a story in itself. She believes it was miraculous and the doctors and physical therapists are astonished. Gwen was released from physical therapy in record time with no major problems. When I saw her return to work, I expected to see a limp or a grimace of pain. There was nothing but her shining face and big smile. I could tell the splinter she'd had in her heart weeks ago was gone. She was glowing with God's love evident in her. She says there's just a little stiffness and believes with all her heart all that will go away. She exercises daily and is determined to be completely healthy. For now it's amazing to look at someone who was hit by a car weeks earlier have no limp, have no pain, and not be on any kind of pain medicine. Gwen excitedly tells her story of healing. She says it's been a miracle.

Gwen says she made a peace with God during the first days of her recovery. She realized and accepted this is not her body; she didn't make it and can't help put it back together.

During the weeks at home recovering, Gwen got a chance to do what she loves best: be with her son and paint. That, too, turned into a miraculous work of God. She was in the bed in a chest brace, with an ice pack on her leg and an easel by her bed. She says some of her sheets are still stained with oil paint. Many of her paintings have a religious theme. In her work, she was giving back some of God's love with which she'd been drenched. Those stains are precious to her now. This artist was supposed to participate in three art shows she had agreed to before the accident. God met every need.

Not only did He raise up people to bring her food, He also raised up people to help get her paintings to these shows. She had paintings that needed to be framed, picked up, and delivered. Someone from one of the galleries took care of all the errands.

While she was healing, she was painting. In fact, she turned out a record number of paintings. Gwen had used the talent God gave her to turn out nine paintings during her time off. She ended up entering 26 paintings for the show in December.

With the help of a walker, Gwen attended the December show. She says with the walker she was looking down to steady her steps. But she thought about it and on a daily basis, now that she is free of the walker, she physically looks up to remind herself of God's greatness, power, and love. "We can so easily get stuck on this earth looking down at our problems and struggles. But we must keep our eyes on Him," she reminded me. "I look up to the hills as is mentioned in the Word. Keep looking up."

As for the man who was driving the car that hit Gwen, she said she had to let it go. The man had no insurance and couldn't help Gwen pay for her bills while she was off from work. Friends and neighbors told her she should take the man to court. She would reply, "God took care of my every need right down to someone bringing hay for my horse; so suing would be like slapping God in the face for all He has given me."

There are a lot of lessons Gwen learned through this horrendous accident. But one she says that is so clear is that God will provide for every need.

Gwen said with excitement. "I would get a bill in the mail or wonder how I would take care of something and within a few minutes the need was met by someone. I can see how He is growing me and teaching me to trust Him. As time went by, the needs were still coming and the time He would take to answer that need became a little bit longer and a little bit longer. Now I realize, He's just telling me to trust Him in all things, and I do!" She smiled with youthful enthusiasm.

"I have given you authority over all the power of the enemy, and you can walk among snakes and scorpions and crush them. Nothing will injure you."
—Luke 10:19

Many weeks later, when she walked into work to return to her job as a graphic artist, she tells me she walked in as a different person, a transformed person. The angry, hurt person that felt so alone and unloved was gone. God transformed her by His love. He showed her His love through so many people. These were all people Gwen considered friends, acquaintances, and people with whom she worked. But God opened her eyes through her accident; that she is loved by many and most importantly loved by Him, her Father in heaven!

His Love Keeps Us on Track

Does God tell us we have a choice to choose cheerfulness over a crushed spirit? You bet. Do I do it consistently? Nope. I try to get back on track. I ask Him to help me.

> *A cheerful heart is good medicine, but a broken spirit saps a person's strength.*
>
> —Proverbs 17:22

I try to remember to accept and submit to the Lord's plan. We will be amazed by His grace and glory when we do. I've truly been blessed even though I didn't plan to get sick and never wanted to experience grief or heartache. I can see how the Lord is growing me through adversity and people like my friend Gwen.

As I mentioned in a previous chapter, sometimes it's hard to get past the mirror image of what has happened in our lives. Who that person is and what that person lost and what that person in the reflection needs. Satan wants to deceive us and keep us from accessing the true power that God has for us. His power operates through love. We don't have a big, mean, torturing God; we have a loving God who wants the best for us. By focusing on God's light past the mirror, He will raise us to new heights we could never imagine.

> *"The joy of the LORD is your strength!"*
>
> —Nehemiah 8:10

Praise God for His love and wisdom. Remember, when you are experiencing heartache, how much more Christ endured on the cross suffering for our sins. He died so that we could live. Don't pass up the gift He's provided you. Our slates are wiped clean. You are able to be cleansed by His blood. You are healed by His stripes—even your soul's diseases from sin—and you have been set free if you choose to accept that freedom. Simply receive Him in your heart, acknowledge you are a sinner—as we are all from birth—and hold on the ride of your life. The Lord has plans for you!

> *"For I know the plans I have for you," declares the* LORD, *"plans to prosper you and not to harm you, plans to give you hope and a future."*
> —Jeremiah 29:11 (NIV)

Sometimes those plans are fulfilled here on earth and sometime the full healing takes place in heaven. But while we are here we are commanded to love each other and care for one another and pray for healing for one another.

Recently, my husband was perusing the sports page in Charlotte, North Carolina. During the basketball season, he travels there to work for ESPN. He's the studio host for the Big 12 and a play-by-play announcer. While eating his complimentary breakfast alone at the hotel one morning in Charlotte, he grabbed his morning companion, the newspaper. An article caught his eye with a headline that read, "Cancer battle hasn't dimmed her faith."

It was a story about the North Carolina State women's basketball coach battling her breast cancer. Kay Yow has a determined spirit and says there are still a lot of things she wants to do here, so she's fighting to stick around as long as possible. What hit me about her struggle is that God clearly raised up many people to encourage her and show her His love. Former charismatic NC State National Championship men's basketball coach Jim Valvano talked with her about basketball and the Bible. He even delivered a huge meal from one of his favorite Italian restaurants shortly after her surgery. She admitted she had trouble mustering the energy and was hurting. She wanted to tell him to forget the meal. But she loved her friend and he made her laugh. In fact, it even hurt to laugh. But she did anyway for two hours during their visit.

While Kay's mother and Kay's friend lost their cancer battles in the late nineties, Yow reaches up to God for her strength. Friends describe her as a light, a shining light. She's an inspiration for the girls who know her and everyone she encounters. She eagerly shares the verse that helps her go on. By now, you know that is one of my favorites. "I can do all things through Christ who strengthens me" (Philippians 4:13 NKJV).

Kay Yow asks people to pray. In the *Charlotte Observer* article, it said she asks for the prayer to be directed to her doctors that they can find the right way to treat her and others. Even in her own struggle, she is showing her love for others.

Even in the times we are hurting the most, God moves people to show their love for us by delivering meals, telling us jokes, making us laugh. He did that for me. There were times after my surgery that it hurt to breathe. But there was that wonderful friend's voice on the other end of the telephone making me laugh. Or there was James Spann and his lovely wife, Karen, showing up in my hospital room with big smiles encouraging me. When God moves you to encourage someone, don't hesitate. I would get an encouraging word the minute I had a doubt. The very minute I started to go into a pit of depression or feel like I couldn't go on, there was someone there to provide the exact answer to my question with a specific Bible verse. Just like He did Gwen, who was hit by a car, and Kay Yow, in her battle with stage-four cancer, God raises up His people to show His love.

The great news is God loves you no matter what. You don't have to be perfect for Him to love you. He loves all of us equally. So if you've ever felt second fiddle in your family, the good news is you are not second fiddle with God. He loves you even when you sin, or mess up. He loves you when you don't feel like you love yourself. You are precious to Him and important enough for Him to die for! When you don't feel like you have a friend, like the old hymn says, you have a friend in Jesus. He wants a relationship with you.

I'm still surprised and in awe that He answers specific prayers. I was praying for and wondering about a man I had prayed for healing. I said, "Lord, I just have to know how Mr. King is." I prayed that he would be healed from cancer. I had tried to get in touch with him but had no way of finding him. A few days after that prayer, guess who calls? It was Mr. King after a year and a half, out of the blue. God loves us and wants us to love and encourage one another. We can experience His kingdom here on earth by accessing and accepting His love in our lives and using that love to His glory. Love, if you think about it, is powerful. Love can make the difference in someone having the will to fight to be healed. Even if you feel alone, God wants you to know you are His and He is there every step of the way. God loves you and I do too! Pass it on!

> *Dear friends, let us love one another, for love comes from God. Everyone who loves has been born of God and knows God. Whoever does not love does not know God, because God is love. This is how God showed his love among us: He sent his one and only Son into the world that we might live through him. This is love: not that we loved God, but that he loved us and sent his Son as an atoning sacrifice for our sins. Dear friends, since God so loved us, we also ought to love one*

another. No one has ever seen God; but if we love one another, God lives in us and his love is made complete in us.

We know that we live in him and he in us, because he has given us of his Spirit. And we have seen and testify that the Father has sent his Son to be the Savior of the world. If anyone acknowledges that Jesus is the Son of God, God lives in him and he in God. And so we know and rely on the love God has for us.

God is love. Whoever lives in love lives in God, and God in him. In this way, love is made complete among us so that we will have confidence on the day of judgment, because in this world we are like him. There is no fear in love. But perfect love drives out fear, because fear has to do with punishment. The one who fears is not made perfect in love.

We love because he first loved us. If anyone says, "I love God," yet hates his brother, he is a liar. For anyone who does not love his brother, whom he has seen, cannot love God, whom he has not seen. And he has given us this command: Whoever loves God must also love his brother.

—1 John 4:7–21 (NIV)

Worship Study Questions

• How does God show me His love?

_____

_____

_____

_____

• Which Scriptures remind me that He is always there and always loving me?

_____

_____

_____

_____

•. How is God moving me to show my love for others?

_____

_____

_____

_____

• How can I use love to defeat a negative situation in my life?

_____

_____

_____

_____